FROM **PONY** TO **UNICORN**

'Blitzscaling a start-up to a [sustainable] unicorn is a feat that very few have managed for good reason—it's like riding the proverbial tiger. *From Pony to Unicorn* is an engaging book filled with real-life stories that will be valuable to every entrepreneur who hopes to successfully do this.'—Ravi Venkatesan, member of the board of trustees, Rockefeller Foundation, and founder, Global Alliance for Mass Entrepreneurship

'*From Pony to Unicorn* is a collection of insights on different aspects of scaling based on real-life experiences. Sanjeev and Hari have been through this journey multiple times and they have shared stories based on their own experiences as well as those of other entrepreneurs. This is a must-read for anyone trying to build and scale a business sustainably.'—Deep Kalra, founder and CEO, MakeMyTrip

'*From Pony to Unicorn* is a fascinating read about a playbook for sustainable growth for any start-up. Hari and Sanjeev draw striking parallels between religion, science, humans and start-ups to chronicle the journey of scale. An insightful and important read for anyone thinking of resetting their business, or life!'—Ashni Biyani, managing director, Future Consumer

'The book illustrates the different components of scale, and the levers available to founders, with real examples and stories. Sanjeev and Hari have seen, from close quarters, several start-ups scale to become large companies. I would recommend the book as a must-read for entrepreneurs and investors.'—Sanjeev Bikhchandani, founder and executive vice chairman, Naukri

'The book brings out powerful insights on the principles behind scaling. Sanjeev and Hari have been through this journey several times. The Indian start-up and business ecosystem needed a book like this that brings out insights through real-life experiences, anecdotes and events that shaped the scale journeys of start-ups. I would recommend this as a must-read for anyone involved in scaling a start-up.'—K. Ganesh, serial entrepreneur and chairman, GrowthStory

'There is a lot of wisdom in this book that comes from being practitioners. A great book not just for founders and entrepreneurs but also for leaders in general.'—T.V. Narendran, global CEO and managing director, Tata Steel

'Hari and Sanjeev have crunched multiple decades of experience, learning and insights into a book than can act as a ready reckoner for all entrepreneurs.

I wish I had access to this book during my scaling days! The book is a must-read for all the founders and leadership teams of start-ups who are on their scaling journey.'—Raghunandan G., co-founder, TaxiForSure

'*From Pony to Unicorn* is a book about the x to 10x journey. Hari and Sanjeev have been through this journey several times. The book lucidly brings out the principles behind scaling. The book is easy to read, and full of real-life anecdotes and insights. I would recommend this as a must-read for every entrepreneur, leader and investor involved in scaling a start-up.' —Vishal Gupta, managing director, Bessemer Venture Partners

'The book targets the heart of why India is poor; we have too many enterprises that are dwarfs, not babies. It wonderfully unpacks the difference between a recipe and list of ingredients for enterprises that scale. Every entrepreneur needs a hearing aid, and this book is important reading for anybody who wants to create India calibration scale.'—Manish Sabharwal, chairman, TeamLease Services

'I have had the good fortune of seeing Daksh as well as BigBasket scale and experience their "scale" mindset. This book is a treasure trove of lessons and case studies of that mindset by two successful business leaders. *From Pony to Unicorn* is a masterclass in entrepreneurship.'—Deep Mukherjee, senior vice president, corporate, Star TV Network

'*From Pony to Unicorn* is a delightful book on the 1–10 journey of a start-up, and Hari and Sanjeev bring a deep understanding of scaling start-ups, having gone through this journey themselves several times over. The insights are powerful and the book is a great guide for any entrepreneur or leader who is involved in scaling their start-up. Recommend this strongly!' —Shradha Sharma, founder and CEO, YourStory

'*From Pony to Unicorn* is a book about the journey of a start-up after the product–market fit has been established. The book lucidly brings out the principles behind scaling. Sanjeev and Hari have been through this journey several times and it reflects in the real-life anecdotes and insights. I would recommend this as a must-read for every entrepreneur, leader and investor involved in scaling a start-up.'—Dharmil Seth, co-founder and CEO, Pharmeasy

'The book illustrates the different elements of scaling at start-ups and draws parallels from other walks of life too. Sanjeev and Hari have identified the different levers available to founders and illustrated these with real examples and stories. It is a good read for all entrepreneurs, investors and leaders at start-ups.'—Hari Menon, co-founder and CEO, BigBasket

FROM PONY *TO* UNICORN

SCALING A START-UP SUSTAINABLY

SANJEEV AGGARWAL
T.N.HARI

FOREWORD BY **NANDAN NILEKANI**

PORTFOLIO
PENGUIN

An imprint of Penguin Random House

PORTFOLIO

USA | Canada | UK | Ireland | Australia
New Zealand | India | South Africa | China

Portfolio is part of the Penguin Random House group of companies
whose addresses can be found at global.penguinrandomhouse.com

Published by Penguin Random House India Pvt. Ltd
7th Floor, Infinity Tower C, DLF Cyber City,
Gurgaon 122 002, Haryana, India

First published in Portfolio by Penguin Random House India 2020

Copyright © Sanjeev Aggarwal and T.N. Hari 2020
Foreword © Nandan Nilekani 2020

All rights reserved

10 9 8 7 6 5 4 3 2

The views and opinions expressed in this book are the authors' own and the
facts are as reported by them which have been verified to the extent possible,
and the publishers are not in any way liable for the same.

ISBN 9780670094448

Typeset in Sabon by Manipal Technologies Limited, Manipal
Printed at Replika Press Pvt. Ltd, India

www.penguin.co.in

Dedication by Sanjeev Aggarwal:

I'd like to dedicate this book to my wife Shikha who gave up her dreams to let me pursue mine

Dedication by T.N. Hari:

For V.S. Sudhakar—a karmayogi and an entrepreneur

Contents

Foreword

I have known Sanjeev and Hari for some years now, and I can say with some confidence that they know a thing or two about building scale companies.

From Pony to Unicorn is a book that describes different components of scale and the levers that founders have for growing their start-ups sustainably. Becoming a unicorn is not the goal, as the title might seem to suggest. The goal is to build and grow your start-up based on sound business principles. Your start-up may or may not grow into a unicorn, and quite frankly, that is not even a meaningful goal to have.

The Indian start-up ecosystem has evolved rapidly and become mature in the last two decades. However, funding and valuations have received far more focus and headlines than is healthy. While the positive side of this is that it provides the incentive for entrepreneurs to pursue more audacious ideas, the downside is that it communicates a message to budding entrepreneurs and the community at large that the quality of your business is only determined by the funding you receive or the valuations you command. This belief, and the behaviours it drives, has resulted in some start-ups rapidly getting to the unicorn status but equally rapidly falling off the cliff to be sold off at a fraction of their peak value.

The good news is that there are several start-ups that are seriously pursuing the path of building and growing their businesses sustainably. Founders and leaders at such start-ups will find this book full of real examples and practical tips. The authors have extensively drawn from their own experiences as well as from the experiences of other entrepreneurs who have built successful businesses.

The chapter titled 'Organization DNA' describes with a lot of real examples why culture matters such a great deal. It illustrates how you can create the right culture in your start-up and also describes what culture is not. The chapter 'A Founder's Journey' captures the lessons that founders go through on their journey, which young founders can use to get a glimpse of what awaits them. The lessons here can help them anticipate and prepare in advance without having to learn by making the same mistakes. While some lessons are best learnt by making mistakes, it is not a great idea to make this the sole approach to learning.

In the last few years, the phrase 'Go Big or Go Home' has gained attention. Popularized in Silicon Valley in the dot-com era, this is not necessarily a good guiding principle for founders. The authors have addressed this in the chapter titled, 'The Alternative to "Go Big" Cannot Be "Go Home"'.

Making the right strategic choices at each stage of the journey as well as making the right pivots at the inflection points can be almost make or break for a start-up, and this is illustrated well with examples. The different nuances of human capital and the implications on sustainable growth are extensively addressed.

And the icing on the cake is the last chapter, which is a list of ten good habits that form the foundation of building any business the right way.

I have personally been deeply involved in different capacities in building scale organizations. Each case was different and unique in some ways, but at a different level, some of the underlying principles were all the same. Whether it was building Infosys or Aadhaar, some of the principles of scale were common. As I read through the book, I could relate to many of the lessons that have been presented.

The book is full of interesting anecdotes that make for easy reading while beautifully bringing out some of the principles in a simple and easy-to-understand way. There are lessons in it for everyone: investors, entrepreneurs and employees.

I would strongly recommend this book to anyone interested in building a sustainable business.

—Nandan Nilekani
Chairman, Infosys and Chairman,
Fundamentum Partnership

1

The Road to Scale

Happy families are all alike; every unhappy family is unhappy in its own way.

—Leo Tolstoy, in *Anna Karenina*

In his epochal book, *Small Is Beautiful*, Ernst Friedrich Schumacher says, 'Even today, we are generally told that gigantic organizations are inescapably necessary; but when we look closely we can notice that as soon as great size has been created there is often a strenuous attempt to attain smallness within bigness.' Big companies have tried to act small to preserve innovation. Extreme proportions, whether for a life form or an organization, is not natural. It is only in science fiction that one comes across animals the size of Godzilla. The network of blood vessels and nerves and the bone structures needed to support a life form of this size don't exist in the real world. Even large organizations need intricate structures, speedy communication channels,

1

an extremely strong foundation and flawless management. From time to time, a few organizations defy all odds and make it really big until a small start-up somewhere ends up disrupting them.

However, the quest for scale is never-ending. One of the most enduring human pursuits throughout history has been to create things on a grand scale. Whether it was building mammoth pyramids in Egypt or connecting the Mediterranean with the Red Sea through the Suez, or laying undersea cables across the Atlantic, the attraction for grandeur and scale has been incessant.

Despite the obsessive and timeless allure of scale, the failure rate has been high. Failure to scale can be because of many reasons, some of which are quite universal and pervasive. They show up in almost every scaling scenario. An understanding of these reasons can be very helpful. It does not guarantee success but can raise the odds in favour of success appreciably. There are also unique challenges in every scaling scenario. You need to deal with these like you would deal with any 'first time' problem.

Tolstoy's quote from *Anna Karenina* is beautiful and sublime, but there are underlying nuances and variations in its meaning. It is the sheer variety and number of nuances that make universal prescriptions for success and scaling, as much as for happiness, almost impossible and often meaningless. This applies as much to start-ups as to families. The closest universal prescription for success was from Arthur Rubinstein, who once said, 'There is no formula for success, except perhaps an unconditional acceptance of life and what it brings.' Insights and prescriptions make sense only to individuals who recognize deeply that lessons and wisdom are meaningless in the absence of context, and there is no wisdom or prescription that can't be challenged. However, given a clear context, an insight drawn from similar contexts can be very powerful, create those 'Aha!' moments and help you rapidly overcome the hurdle that is holding you back.

Steve Blank, a highly respected author on entrepreneurship in Silicon Valley, in an interview with Kevin Ready published by *Forbes* magazine, defines a start-up as a 'temporary organization designed to search for a repeatable and scalable business model'. Eric Ries, a successful American entrepreneur and prolific author, in his seminal book *The Lean Start-up*, defines a start-up as an organization that is dedicated to creating something new under conditions of extreme uncertainty. He further adds, 'this is just as true for one person in a garage as it is for a group of seasoned professionals in a Fortune 500 boardroom. What they have in common is a mission to penetrate that fog of uncertainty to discover a successful path to a sustainable business'. This is a reasonably accurate description of what every start-up sets out to do. However, it is a bit too broad and would include many organizations, such as research laboratories and Fortune 100 companies that wouldn't be considered start-ups. Therefore, let's narrow this down by adding three other unambiguous filters before an organization dedicated to creating something new under conditions of extreme uncertainty can be called a start-up: a) the founder/s should still be active; b) it should be funded by venture capital (VC); and c) it should still be a private company. If these filters are applied, companies like Amazon, Google, Flipkart, Uber and Lyft would fail to qualify as start-ups, while BigBasket, DoorDash, Rubrick, Dunzo, Paytm and Swiggy would all qualify. While founder/s being active and the start-up not yet being a public company are understandable filters, the additional filter of the organization being VC-funded is relevant because that helps exclude mom-and-pop businesses that don't have the same appetite for scaling as VC-funded start-ups.

Caveat: For Every Prescription, the Opposite Could Be Equally True

Every insight has a flip side. This applies not just to management insights but to the most common wisdom dished out as idioms. While curiosity may have killed the cat, everyone understands that it is essential for innovation and progress. Therefore, bereft of context, no maxim or insight is relevant.

Blitzkrieg is a method of warfare popularized in Europe after World War I where through a swift and concentrated attack on an enemy's strategic assets and positions, a war could be won at lightning speed. Some founders backed by like-minded investors adopted this strategy in a different battlefield where 'capital' was the equivalent of tanks and aircraft in a blitzkrieg strategy. This strategy in the scaling context has not been without its critics. Many have argued that overcapitalization can hide inefficiencies and a poor product–market fit. However, there have been enough cases where overcapitalized start-ups were able to replicate the success of a blitzkrieg approach by racing away to scale and emerge as near monopolies (or part of a duopoly) by successfully forcing competitors to shut. In such an approach, the product–market fit was attained by continuous tweaks along the way. Start-ups like Uber,

Ola, Didi Chuxing and Oyo are a few examples. This still does not mean that after achieving a monopoly/duopoly status, all these businesses were extremely profitable or attractive by public market benchmarks. In a few cases, they were profitable and listed successfully too. In many others, the markets that these well-capitalized start-ups created by liberal deployment of capital were inherently unsustainable and shrunk after they made a serious attempt to address profitability issues. So, the growth–profit dichotomy or the overcapitalization-versus-optimal-capitalization debate could go on for ever with no right or wrong answers. It is the context that decides what is relevant. We will discuss these in the chapters titled, 'Alternative to "Go Big" Cannot Be "Go Home"' and 'Capitalization and Valuations'.

Similarly, there is a view that first movers have a huge advantage in some industries, especially in the consumer Internet space. It is believed that in markets with a strong 'network effect', there is a decisive advantage of being the first mover. Even in other markets, the first-mover advantage is strong, if not decisive. Coca Cola, Kellogg's and Apple are examples of first movers which continue to be way ahead of the second mover in their respective industries. In contrast, Google, Facebook and Amazon are examples of huge successes despite not being first movers (Google was not even among the first ten search engines!). And these are examples of late movers emerging as undisputed leaders in a space where early movers were expected to have an unassailable lead. You will of course have someone explain away that Facebook ultimately eclipsed Friendster, Orkut and Myspace because it did not think about monetization until the user base increased significantly whereas Friendster and Myspace began driving monetization a tad prematurely.

Another common debate is whether to pivot or persevere. Both start-ups as well as large and mature companies go through inflection points and pivots, when near-perfect product–market fits begin to get challenged by new developments. Seemingly invincible giants have been successfully challenged by fledgling start-ups, especially in the tech industry. While some of these giants pivoted successfully to stay in the game, others just lost the plot. The decline was swift for those who lost the plot. We will discuss this in the chapter titled, 'Inflection Points and Pivots'.

There has also been a good amount of debate on the leadership traits of founders and founder CEOs that are best correlated with seamless scaling. But look around and you will find sufficient examples that can bust any attempt at a hasty generalization. There have been similar debates about a seasoned leadership team versus a team with a strong leader supported by a bunch of doers. Lateral hires versus internal promotions, too few or too many laterals, hiring above or below, generalists or specialists, learning while you scale, dealing with underperformers, effectiveness of incentive plans—these are all important questions.

Diversity in leadership—or even diversity across the board—versus having a homogeneous leadership team is another silent and rarely acknowledged debate. There are successful examples of both. But look a little harder and deeper and you may discover that what took a start-up from zero to one, for instance, may not take it from, say, one to ten, or even prove to be its nemesis in this leg of the journey. And this holds true for all other parameters as much as for diversity. So, when to flip is key. But making a flip isn't easy, as one might imagine, even if one understands the need for this flip. The reason is quite obvious: Old habits die hard, and old habits also often reflect the deep personal beliefs of a founder, which are difficult to change.

We will discuss all these topics in some detail in the chapters 'The Human Capital' and 'A Founder's Journey'.

There is also the discussion around 'culture' and the interesting questions it throws up. Is there a good and a bad culture? Is culture change possible? Is it top-down or bottom-up? Is there a desirable culture that every start-up should aspire for? Why is it that one hears so many negative things about Amazon's pressure cooker kind of aggressive culture, and yet the company continues to be the leader in its chosen field of e-commerce? Does culture really impact business, and if yes, how do you make it work for you rather than against you? We will discuss this in the chapter titled 'Organization DNA'.

Any attempt at generalization should also keep in mind the culture of the nation in which the organization is headquartered, the political compulsions, the nature of governments, the structure of the economy, and a host of other factors. We will address a bit of this in the third chapter where we will try and draw some comparisons between the US, China and India, the three largest economies in 'purchasing power parity' (PPP) terms.

The Highway to Scale Is Not Straight

There are multiple hairpin bends along the way, and the skills needed to navigate each bend are not necessarily the same as those that were helpful in navigating the previous bend. For instance, reputation management may not be essential for survival at an early stage but at a late stage this can be make or break. Therefore, by the time a start-up reaches late-stage, the founders should have learnt the art of building and managing reputation by creating a coalition of diverse allies to pre-emptively employ soft power, especially during a crisis. And this is a crucial capability the start-up must plan for and build proactively. Therefore, leadership teams, especially the founders, need to learn rapidly along the way. Unfortunately, most of these learnings are experiential and are cemented after making mistakes.

Every start-up has its own set of unique hairpin bends or discontinuities. It is even more difficult, as an insider, to anticipate an upcoming discontinuity and prepare for it because the signals are not unambiguous. The reason why intelligence agencies find it so difficult to pre-empt many terrorist strikes, including the 9/11 attack, is that low-intensity signals that point to a terrorist plot are always present. However, acting on every indicator without adequate triangulation and validation can create false alarms and ultimately divert, engage and lock-in precious resources. The difficulties in spotting a genuine upcoming discontinuity are somewhat similar. The signal is never strong and unambiguous enough to be spotted by an untrained eye.

To add to the twist, the discontinuities that one start-up goes through along its maturity journey can be very different from what another start-up goes through. Nonetheless, it is not impossible to define and characterize some of these discontinuities. Based on what we have seen and experienced, we can come up with a list. But whenever, in the past, we tried doing this, we discovered that our list ended up looking eerily similar to a model that Larry Greiner had described in an article in the July–August 1972 issue of the *Harvard Business Review* titled 'Evolution and Revolution as Organizations Grow'. This once again reinforced our belief that pretty much anything that matters in any domain, except in cutting-edge scientific research, has already been discovered, understood, articulated, commented upon and eventually forgotten. Only to be rediscovered serendipitously by someone else. Galileo once said, 'All truths are easy to understand once they are discovered. The point is to discover them.' If there is one reason why reading is a good habit, it is because it raises the probability of discovering some powerful truths and learning something without going through the torment of painfully reinventing the wheels in your life.

The summary of Greiner's model is that as a start-up scales rapidly and tries to remain innovative, it begins to spin out of control a bit and this jeopardizes its pursuit of growth and efficiency. Therefore, to keep the centrifugal forces in check and stay as one piece, it needs to begin instituting a slew of stabilizing mechanisms like process, procedure, protocol and compliance at every level in the organization. This tends to introduce bureaucracy at the cost of innovation and agility. The stabilizing mechanisms could eventually begin to overpower the forces of disruption, and by the time they get to the final stage, many companies tend to become conservative, short-sighted and contented with their past successes. Over the course of time, some of them see flattening of growth and a slow decline. Very few are able to reinvent themselves by making the necessary changes in culture, structure and leadership to continue to remain innovative.

Rapid scaling, without the wheels coming off, needs the founders to demonstrate the kind of learning that is nothing short of a five-year-old child starting with elementary math and graduating to calculus by the age of ten. Not many children can do this.

Lessons to Be Learnt from Failure to Scale

'Or' and 'and' are two of the many 'Logic Gates' in Boolean algebra. Everyone knows that the 'or' gate is far easier to fulfil than the 'and' gate because the former needs just **one** of the many conditions to be met whereas the latter requires **all** the conditions to be met. Success is like the 'and' gate, where multiple conditions need to come together at different stages, while failure is more often like the 'or' gate where just one fatal flaw is all that is needed. A large part of success (outside of sheer chance) is being able to avoid these errors at the turning points. However, one can also argue that if a start-up gets a few strategic choices right, it can live with a few flaws as long as any of these flaws are not fatal.

We believe that failure to scale offers as many, if not more, lessons on how to scale successfully. We will therefore discuss a few examples of start-ups that failed to scale in subsequent chapters.

Powerful Lessons for Scaling from Other Contexts

Lessons for scaling can be drawn from other fields as well and can be as effective. Religion has always been a mystery to people with a strong scientific or business bent of mind. But there are great parallels to be drawn from how some religions scaled rapidly.

Let's take a look at why Christianity scaled and spread like wildfire in the ancient world, and the lessons it has for scaling start-ups.

Christianity was beginning to grow in substantial ways by the late second and early third centuries precisely because it was responding to some basic and deeply felt human need. It was solving a real problem. In spite of all the glories of the Roman Empire, people lived in a world in which there was inequality, poverty and extreme concentration of wealth. There was sickness and disease, and no public health services. Rome had a very hierarchical system and if you were at the bottom of that social pyramid (slaves and widows), life was torture. In a time when the Roman Empire was corrupt and decadent, Christianity offered a sense of community.

Christian churches established hospitals and schools for the poor and an institution for widows, because a woman who had lost her husband and did not have money of her own was at the very bottom of the social ladder in Roman society. Christianity introduced the value of humility in a society where hubris was the norm.

As the church developed, it allowed for different degrees of Christian devotion. You would be glorified if you decided to renounce everything and gave yourself up to a highly ascetic life. However, you could also be married, have a family, a career and a position, and that was all right too. So Christianity could adjust itself to different types of people, just as it could adjust itself to the highest class of intellectuals and also to common people (the equivalent of a large Total Addressable Market or TAM).

Christianity might have remained a strictly Jewish sect if it were not for one man, Saul, who was considered the 'father of Christianity'. Saul was also referred to as Paul, though there are many conflicting views on whether he always had two names like some Jews or whether he changed his name to Paul after becoming a follower of Jesus Christ. This is beside the point, though. Saul soon converted to Christianity and dedicated his life to spreading the new religion. Without him, Christianity may not have become a prominent religion in the Roman Empire.

And finally, because of a variety of reasons, Emperor Constantine I, also known as Constantine the Great, chose to support Christianity, and this was the tipping point.

There are all the elements in this story that a rapidly scaling start-up cares for: solving a deeply felt problem, a large TAM, maniacal focus on the customer, making the right pivots based on market feedback, dealing with competition, opening up new markets with low competitive intensity, having an evangelical leader, and, above all, creating the right culture and standing by it in difficult times.

Panasonic Drew Its Inspiration for Scaling from Religion

Sometime in 1932, Konosuke Matsushita, the founder of Panasonic, spent a day visiting the head temple of a popular religious sect on the invitation of an acquaintance. He was struck by the sight of many followers energetically at work without the matching monetary incentives, which are seen as absolutely essential in the corporate world, to drive this behaviour. As he thought over his impressions, he saw a parallel between the services that religion and business offer to humanity. This is well documented in the stories of Matsushita and the company he founded. Based on this insight, this is how he defined Panasonic's mission:

> Human beings need both physical and spiritual prosperity. Religion is a holy pursuit that guides people out of suffering toward happiness and peace of mind. Business, too, can be sacred in that it can provide the physical necessities required for human happiness. This should be the primary mission of business.

A mission like this helped Panasonic bounce back at the end of every near-death moment it faced in its scaling journey.

AMUL Is an Example of Successful Scaling in another Context

In 1976, a movie titled *Manthan*, produced and directed by one of India's legendary film-makers, Shyam Benegal, was screened in Gujarat. The film, financed through a token contribution from members of the AMUL cooperative, was a roaring success. It was subsequently screened nationally and received a lot of critical acclaim. It won several national awards and was also nominated for the Oscars.

The film told the story of India's White Revolution, more popularly known as 'Operation Flood'. And the man behind it: Verghese Kurien.

This was a classic case of spectacular scaling in a very difficult and unconventional context. The problem that Kurien solved was extremely complex. It addressed three independent objectives: a) massive increase in milk production in the country, b) augmentation of rural incomes, c) reasonable and fair price for end consumers. The second and third objectives were almost in direct conflict, and Amul eventually met each of these two objectives without compromising the other. No entrepreneur saw an opportunity in this problem! And no VC would have been ready to fund it because of the hundreds of moving parts and interdependency involved. But the success that this mission achieved was so stunning that India transformed from a milk-deficit nation to a milk-surplus nation. It transformed the lives of millions of milk farmers in Gujarat to start with, and over time the entire country.

The success in this case is attributable to the grit, tenacity and belief of two extraordinary individuals, namely, Tribhuvandas Patel, the selfless leader of farmers, freedom fighter and the first chairman of Amul, and his protégé, Kurien. The lesson in this for scaling start-ups is that a clear mission and a visionary leader with a strong penchant for execution can truly make all the difference.

In Conclusion

The Rev. Dr Dale Turner, who espoused a liberal Christian doctrine, is quoted by multiple sources as having said, 'Some of the best lessons we ever learn are learned from past mistakes. The error of the past is the wisdom and success of the future.' Lessons on scaling too are best learnt from the mistakes of scaling.

However, organizations are like organisms and cities. They follow certain broad principles of scaling. They reach their pinnacle and die. 'Creative Destruction' is as important an enabler of innovation in organizations as it is in organisms. The churn in the Fortune 500 list is increasing. In a blogpost titled, 'Fortune 500 firms in 1955 vs. 2014; 88% are gone, and we're all better off because of that dynamic "creative destruction"', Mark J. Perry, an American economist and professor of economics and finance at the School of Management at University of Michigan–Flint, wrote that of the Fortune 500 companies in 1955, only 12 per cent survived in 2014, and the half-life of public companies in the US was just ten years. In other words, of all the companies that list in any year, 50 per cent of them vanish in ten years (either through acquisition or death)!

JPMorgan Chase in their research on small businesses found that in 2014, over 99 per cent of America's nearly 30 million firms were small businesses. The vast majority of these employed fewer than twenty people, and nearly 40 per cent of all enterprises had under $100k in revenue. India is not very different. On 23 March 2020, the *Financial Express* reported that, 'according to the MSME ministry's FY19 annual report, the MSME sector is dominated by micro-enterprises. Of the 6.33 crore MSMEs, a staggering 6.3 crores (99.4%) are microenterprises'. The 'middle' is completely missing in India. A vast majority of them do not even have a website.

One of the most universal laws of nature is the law of increasing entropy. It is this law that drives the arrow of time in the forward direction. It dictates that the entropy of the universe will continue to increase, though there are closed entities where the entropy could decrease temporarily. But every closed entity with decreasing entropy is up against this universal law, and every passing day is a losing battle until there is a course correction towards higher entropy and equilibrium. A large organization is one such low-entropy closed entity that is in a state of constant disequilibrium. Building for scale is up against this universal law. Therefore, something is very likely to break as you scale. The laws of probability are stacked against everything coming together to create and sustain this large organization. A single case of sexual harassment, a single large accident, an inadvertent toxic mutation of culture, the exit of a few key leaders, a regulatory trip up, or anything equivalent, is all it could take to cut the ground from under the feet of this organization that is scaling.

Geoffrey West in his seminal book *Scale*, published by Penguin Press in May 2017, points out that scaling laws, whether for organizations, organisms or cities, are consequences of the optimization of network structures that sustain these various systems, resulting from the continuous feedback mechanisms inherent in natural selection and survival of the fittest. There is compelling evidence, even though there are the rare exceptions, that scaling of organizations follows certain power laws. He also points out that after growing rapidly in their youth, almost all companies end up floating on top of the ripples of the stock market with their metaphorical noses just above the surface. This is a precarious situation because they can drown in the next wave, and they are even more vulnerable if they can't deal with the uncertainties of the markets and their own finances.

While it is important to be optimistic and believe that by doing the right things your start-up could deftly navigate through the labyrinth of challenges, it is equally important to have the wisdom to understand that scale, especially extreme scale, is truly an exception and nature has stacked all the odds against it! With this reality check, we close the first chapter.

2

A Playbook for Scale

We all have what it takes to do exactly what we want to do in life, no matter what anyone else says. If someone tells you, 'You can't do this because you are [fill in the blank],' I say embrace the challenge. Wear it like a new pair of Converse or Jordans. Meet it head-on.

—Kwame Alexander, author of *The Playbook*

We believe there are nine determinants of scale. The odds in favour of scaling and growing into a unicorn increase significantly if all these conditions are met:

1. **Mega trend:** Being in the middle of a mega trend is necessary.
2. **Market opportunity:** Participating in a large market (large TAM) is needed too.
3. **Founder ambition:** Not all founders have this burning ambition. Having it helps.

4. **Foundation:** A strong foundation lowers risk and helps in building reputation.
5. **Strategic choices:** Making the right strategic choices at key points in the journey is vial.
6. **Strategic execution:** What 'not to do' is as important as 'what to do.'
7. **Culture (values driven):** This creates lasting success and helps in institution building.
8. **Customer centricity:** This is key to staying relevant at every stage in the journey.
9. **Human capital programmes:** Hiring, promoting and assimilating talent is critical.

The first two are external to the organization and the remaining seven are internal. To aid memory, the framework can be summarized by the first letters of each determinant: MM-FF-SS-CC-H.

The external determinants of being in the middle of a mega trend with a large market opportunity (TAM) seem like pretty obvious prerequisites for start-ups to scale quickly into large enterprises. At times, a mega trend may not be very obvious or evident and can actually be triggered by a smart entrepreneur. For some, though, the mega trend may only be visible in hindsight. Whether Amazon and Uber spotted a mega trend before it was visible to others or just happened to be the first to execute well in what were obvious mega trends and large markets is a debate worth having. As a rule of thumb (and rules of thumb are just rules of thumb), if a start-up is operating in a space with an addressable market of $10 billion and can realistically aspire for a 5 per cent market share, then it could potentially scale to becoming a unicorn. A 5 per cent market share would result in a revenue of $500 million, and assuming a valuation that is two times the revenue, the valuation is a billion dollars.

Unicorns emerge far more easily in 'winner takes all' markets that are driven by 'network effects'. These are typically in the So-Mo space (social and mobile) where more often than not just one or two players eventually survive. The social and mobile space easily transcends geographical and national boundaries because a) there is not a whole lot of product customization that is needed for different markets; and b) the infrastructure needed is just the Internet and a telecom network, which are now pretty standard and ubiquitous. As a result, transforming the whole world into one big market is not particularly difficult. The first mover does not necessarily have an unequivocal advantage though. The first chapter has a few examples on how late entrants in these markets emerged as undisputed winners. Microsoft also played in a 'winner takes all' field with a very powerful network effect. We have talked about this at length in the chapter, 'Alternative to "Go Big" Cannot Be "Go Home"'.

Unicorns can also emerge in the 'local' market with a highly disaggregated set of service providers. A combination of technology and great execution on the ground can help disrupt such markets. In this scenario, there could be multiple winners. If technology was all it took to disrupt a market like this, then it would have been more conducive for a monopoly or duopoly. It is the additional component of execution on the ground that makes it favourable for multiple winners to emerge. The space of enterprise business too tends to accommodate multiple winners for several reasons. If Citibank picks Infosys as its offshore technology development partner, it's very unlikely that its biggest competitor would also pick Infosys for fear of compromising customer data or strategic insights. They would rather work with another equally big outsourcing partner like TCS. Cloud computing, which is part of the enterprise business space, is settling into a three-player game with Amazon, Google and Microsoft. BlackBerry may have been an exception as most corporates used it at one point of time for their corporate email. No other company offered the same level of data security as BlackBerry did at that point of time. However, BlackBerry was disrupted by a completely different innovation, and we will talk about this aspect in the chapter 'Pivots and Inflection Points'.

When a mega trend and a large TAM come together, it tends to attract 'gorillas', or the large incumbents. Gorillas are, however, not always successful against more nimble entrants, but often have sufficient heft and financial clout to give these new entrants serious pain and agony. Gorillas come in different forms, and one common manifestation is of a 'global player' with an aspiration to participate in any big opportunity across the globe. Uber was the gorilla in urban commute, but Ola successfully tackled it in the Indian market through a combination of great execution, strong founder ambition and an alliance with a gorilla from the investing world (SoftBank). Amazon and Walmart-Flipkart are the two gorillas that BigBasket is dealing with. BigBasket has been continuously outmanoeuvring these two gorillas at every step through a combination of razor-sharp focus on things that matter, terrific execution, and a strategic alliance with another gorilla from the e-commerce world: Alibaba. Gorillas can also come in the form of large and powerful domestic conglomerates like Reliance, which has the potential to disrupt any industry it chooses to enter, including online retail. As this book goes to print, Reliance JioMart has made a foray into online grocery, and one of the questions that keeps getting tossed at us in multiple forums is BigBasket's strategy for dealing with this new gorilla. Our view is that the grocery market in India is likely to touch a trillion dollars by 2025 and is big enough to accommodate some more equally large gorillas. And more players in this space actually make it that much easier to change consumer mindset and behaviour. Large horizontal e-commerce players like Amazon and Walmart-Flipkart are gorillas that not just BigBasket but every single vertical e-commerce player, including Lenskart, Pepperfry and others, needs to contend with and be wary of.

In the online travel and ticketing space, MakeMyTrip (MMT) was competing with Goibibo, which was backed by a big gorilla in the form of Naspers. Deep Kalra, founder of MMT, quickly brought Ctrip, another gorilla, on board and then it became a battle of equals. Eventually, reflecting a need to address poor industry profitability through consolidation, MMT and Goibibo themselves came together in what was at that time the biggest mergers and acquisitions (M&A) deal.

In China, two big gorillas have emerged in the e-commerce space—Alibaba and Tencent. Everyone playing in the e-commerce space seems to ultimately ally with one of these two. The story of taxi aggregation in China is a reflection of the rivalry, and the uneasy truce, between these two gorillas. Didi Dache, after an initial funding of $3 million from GSR Ventures, secured a $15 million Series B investment from Tencent in July 2013. At that time, Didi was competing head on with the Alibaba-backed Kuaidi

Dache. For some years, both engaged in a price war not unlike what happened in India some years later between Ola, TaxiForSure and Uber. Tencent and Alibaba funded the expensive war with their deep pockets. Each announced a $100 million round.

By the end of that year, both companies had earned enough funding to be considered two of China's early unicorns. Didi emerged as the dominant player in this round. In February 2015, Tencent-backed Didi and Alibaba-backed Kuaidi initiated a merger of their two companies. In August 2016, the combined entity, Didi Chuxing, then acquired Uber China for $7 billion. Uber maintained a nearly 20 per cent stake in the company, making it the company's largest shareholder. It was a great deal for Uber. For all the sympathy that Uber garnered in the initial days of its battle with the Chinese combine of Didi Chuxing, they eventually acquired a stake worth $7 billion in their rival by burning through just $2 billion!

Amazon and Hindustan Unilever (HUL) have been formidable gorillas in India. They have successfully dodged and outmanoeuvred other nimble local players consistently. At times, they have had to bite the dust temporarily but have quickly got their act together to fight back and establish supremacy. The reason they have been successful is their ability to decentralize and allow local management complete freedom to make strategic choices. Gorillas with a decentralized approach to making strategic choices, based on local conditions, are the ones that are formidable and need to be feared the most. On the other hand, Rocket Internet was a gorilla that failed badly in India. None of the ventures they funded did well, and Rocket had to eventually quit India lock, stock and barrel.

Founder ambition too comes in many shades. Management guru C.K. Prahalad once said, 'If your aspirations are not greater than your resources, you're not an entrepreneur.' Every start-up that has scaled has been invariably founded and led by entrepreneurs with ambition and imagination. Amazon started off as an online bookstore and could have remained an online bookstore but it went on to do many different things including creating a cloud services platform in the form of Amazon Web Services (AWS). Zomato started off as a platform for restaurant ratings but soon saw the huge opportunity in food delivery, and, despite a delayed start, went on to catch up with Swiggy, which itself is a great example of founder imagination and ambition. BigBasket always stayed ahead of the pack of online grocery players through founder ambition and clarity. Ola raced neck and neck with Uber in India because of strong founder ambition. Ambition and imagination manifested in different forms in each of these cases. It came across as brash in some cases and remained understated in others. For some, founder ambition was about hustling and personally executing strategic initiatives. For others, it was about getting the right organization architecture and delegating. Founder ambition has always benefitted by access to the right kind of mentors. These mentors help the founders stay anchored. Roger McNamee was a great mentor and advisor to Mark Zuckerberg. He counselled Zuckerberg to not sell Facebook to Yahoo, and to hire Sheryl Sandberg as COO. Later on, of course, McNamee turned out to be a vocal critic of Facebook's 'Privacy Manifesto', which he claimed was a sham and a PR stunt. Similarly, Rajeev Motwani, a Stanford professor, was a great mentor to the

Google founders in the early days. Having such mentors helps channel founder ambition in the right direction and gives it refinement and punch. Sometimes an early client or an early investor could play that role equally effectively. Karthik Reddy, an early investor at TaxiForSure, played that role for Raghunandan G., the co-founder and CEO of TaxiForSure. An early investor in the form of Tiger Global can also end up creating such awe and shock for competition that it can bolster and give wings to founder ambition. Founder ambition has, of course, never been the sole determinant of success and scale. It may seem like a tautology but the truth is that in the absence of this, scale has rarely been attained.

Foundation is the next determinant of scale. In the absence of a strong foundation, there could be short periods of time when one sees scaling but these are mostly false starts that fall flat quickly. Almost every start-up that was funded by Rocket Internet in India falls under this category— Jabong, Foodpanda, among others. There are many global examples too. Rapid scaling without a good product–market fit is also a case of riding on a weak foundation. More often than not, growth without foundation building is a consequence of misplaced founder ambition and overcapitalization. Snapdeal falls under this category. Its repeat rates and Net Promoter Scores (NPS) were low and customer churn was high. Delivery mechanisms were weak and assortment was poor. Customers shopped only for discounts. As Abraham Lincoln once said, 'You can fool all the people some of the time and some people all the time, but you cannot fool all the people all the time.' This is a very apt quote in the context of trying to scale without foundation building. Foundation can be strengthened through a strong and well-intentioned review process that emphasizes the outcomes of foundation building as much as growth or profit goals.

Almost all start-ups that scaled made right strategic choices at key points in their journey. Strategic choices can be on multiple dimensions. They handled the inflection points and pivots well. They also made the right decisions when it came to M&A. Their acquisitions were thoughtful and added strategic value. Myntra, Jabong and Liv.ai were among the strategic acquisitions Flipkart made. Some of these were instrumental in elevating Flipkart into the next orbit. MMT made the right pivot and entered the hotels space. That was the turning point for it. Myntra and Amazon too made the right pivots at the right time. We'll talk about these at length in the chapter 'Pivots and Inflection Points'. Swiggy's decision to focus on supply and operations was a strategic one which helped them get to the pole position in the food-tech race. Both of us worked for a company that one of us (Sanjeev) had co-founded, namely, Daksh. It provided business process outsourcing services to global clients. A strategic choice we made at Daksh was to avoid BOOT deals (build, own, operate and transfer) because eventually when the transfer happened, the revenue fell off the cliff. BOOT contracts were easy to win and if unchecked, the salesforce would end up chasing them. Therefore, we took a conscious call to avoid BOOT deals and got our salesforce to focus on real long-term revenue. At BigBasket, we took the call of going in with a full-stack model, which most big investors like Tiger and SoftBank did not back. But the earth went round the sun even if the pope and the church of the investing world decreed otherwise. Another strategic choice is the extent of capitalization. It is important to be well-capitalized in every phase of growth. Neither overcapitalized nor under-capitalized. In businesses that involve significant cash burn, it is always better to be overcapitalized. Making the right strategic choices is a combination of clear thinking, courage to forego short-term benefits in favour of long-term sustainability, and a penchant for doing the right things for the right reasons. Sometimes, despite all this, even the best choices may not work in the long run. Who said luck does not count!

Strategic execution is the next big lever or determinant of scale. Underneath the big strategic choices, teams need to make the right choices every day in the context of execution. Problem-solving skills and an ability to collaborate help make these choices. Safi Bahcall in his book *Loonshots* calls out two types of innovation, namely, the 'P' type and the 'S' type. The 'P' type innovations are about creating great products that customers absolutely love. Examples are the iPhone and Polaroid cameras, among many others. But the 'S' type involves getting a bunch of seemingly ordinary and interrelated pieces to dovetail in such a perfect way that to an outsider it does not even look like innovation. Every single front-end personnel working in conjunction with process, training and technology to deliver outstanding customer experience in every single interaction is an example of an 'S' type innovation. Almost every single innovation at BigBasket falls under this category. 'S' type innovation is really about strategic execution. Strategic execution is also about knowing what not to do! It is about prioritization and focus. We spoke to Bhaskar Bagchi, who is currently the CEO at OLX Cash My Car. He has been quite remarkable when it comes to executing strategically in every role he has performed. Wherever he has gone, he has woven in elements of customer and business metrics, human capital programmes, and process orientation through a combination of strong reviews and initiatives. For instance, he would use the Gallup12 survey to track and drive employee engagement. Execution is about weaving in these different dimensions seamlessly. As a result, wherever he went, execution was pretty flawless and smooth.

Culture is another crucial determinant of sustained scaling. We will discuss this at length in the chapter titled 'Organization DNA'.

Customer centricity is the other 'C' of scaling. It starts by asking at every stage: 'Why does a customer buy our product or service?' It is about being able to design the product or service based on continuous feedback. It is about being committed to create delight even if it means slowing down the journey a bit or making the right investments ahead of the curve. I was once chatting with Satej Sirur, the co-founder and CEO of Rocketium. He told me that an executive at a big e-commerce company stumped him in a conversation. 'He wanted our API to make millions of product videos but then he started talking about banner images (something we had never done before). I tried my best to steer the conversation back to videos—"videos are so much better", "the world is moving to videos", "our tech is so cool and advanced"—but this did not change anything. The reality was that images were 95 per cent of their need. I went back to the team disappointed that something far simpler than what we had was much more impactful. Once this feeling subsided, the team brainstormed to see what it would take for us to create images. Turns out, our proprietary content format and most of our tech stack could be adapted very easily. Not only that, images could be churned out at 100 times the speed of videos! Twelve months after that fortuitous conversation, images are our fastest growing business and will be the biggest driver of our growth in 2020.' This was a classic case of keeping the customer at the centre of everything.

At BigBasket, the decision to go in for an asset-heavy (or a full-stack) model was based on us answering the question 'Why does a customer shop with BigBasket?' very thoughtfully. The primary reason for a customer to shop at BigBasket was to avoid a visit to the store. What this meant was that if a customer ordered twenty items with us and we could supply only say eighteen, then we would be forcing the customer to visit a physical store for the remaining two items. And, if the customer had to visit a store for these two items, she might as well buy the remaining eighteen from the same store! This helped us realize that a 'fill rate' of near 100 per cent was critical. Not just that, our assortment needed to include fruits, vegetables, as well as chilled and frozen foods. Therefore, we realized the importance of creating the supply chains, which are extremely hard, for these categories.

Human capital is the last and the most obvious determinant of scaling. The nuances are sufficient to discuss this at length in the chapter titled 'The Human Capital'.

In Conclusion

The playbook for scale is at best a broad set of guidelines. Not everyone may even aspire for scale. But for those who do, we believe this playbook provides a broad direction. When ambition is backed up with knowledge of the enablers of scale and some idea of how to deal with them proactively and make them work for you rather than against you, the odds of scaling are multiplied.

3

US, China and India

Don't compare your beginning to someone else's middle.

—Tim Hiller, football coach and author,
Strive—Life is Short

Every organization's story—and every country's history—is unique and different. Comparisons can be odious and often misleading. However, the whole world loves comparisons and seeks to understand what others may be doing differently. They are even keener to understand what successful companies are doing differently. And when it comes to countries, the questions and curiosity are often centred on aspects of culture, history, demography and regulatory frameworks that can explain the paths they have taken and the outcomes they have experienced.

In this chapter, we will talk a little bit about the scaling context and lessons from the world's three largest economies in terms of 'purchasing power parity' (PPP), namely, the US, China and India.

Start-up ecosystems are at best a subset of the larger ecosystem of the economy and the cultural nuances of the country of which they are a part. And the current state of an economy and the cultural fabric of a nation are themselves an outcome of the paths they have traced in history. So, we will briefly touch on some of this before delving into where the Indian start-up ecosystem is in terms of scaling vis-à-vis China and the US.

Scaling in the US: A Brief Historical Context

World War I was the most destructive conflict in human history until World War II (WWII) surpassed it on every conceivable dimension of devastation. The sophistication and destructive power of weapons were several orders of magnitude superior to whatever was used in wars until then. After more than two years of trying to remain neutral, the US, under President Woodrow Wilson, joined the allied powers, Britain, France, Italy and Russia, against the central powers of Germany, Austria-Hungary and Turkey.

In the immediate aftermath of World War I, American and European leaders gathered in Paris to debate and implement far-reaching changes to the pattern of international relations. The 'League of Nations' was established on 16 January 1920. It was seen as the embodiment of a new world order based on mutual cooperation and the peaceful resolution of international conflicts.

Wilson's vision for the post-war world was hugely influential in the founding of the League of Nations. Ironically, the US did not officially join the League of

Nations due to opposition from isolationists in Congress who were opposed to any further US involvement in international conflicts.

Historically, business, much more than geopolitics, has driven the US worldview. The US was considered the epitome of capitalism and individualism. The Great Depression changed this a little bit and the US went on to embrace elements of welfare economics. The blend of capitalism, in its pristine form, and welfare economics along with other ingredients went on to create a terrific recipe for entrepreneurship, innovation and social stability.

Not surprisingly, the League of Nations failed to prevent WWII. The US attitude of staying away from conflict and focusing on business continued until the early stages of WWII when they were blindsided by the sudden and totally unanticipated Japanese attack on Pearl Harbor. This event galvanized the US to take a stand and choose sides. It was also a grim reminder of the fact that staying away from the dirty swamp of geopolitics was not an option. The very wealth it sought to create would be the envy of those who coveted it.

After the end of WWII, the US realized that war itself was great business, and used this insight to great effect in the decades that followed.

The years leading to the culmination of WWII unambiguously established US supremacy in science and technology. The Manhattan Project and the subsequent Apollo programme were some of the high points. The Manhattan Project was the code name of America's secret effort to develop an atomic bomb in response to fears that the Germans were working on using nuclear energy to build a similar bomb and that Adolf Hitler was prepared to use it. The work on the project was undertaken at Los Alamos in New Mexico and not New York as the code name may have suggested. The Apollo programme was designed to land humans on the moon and bring them back safely to earth.

The US welcomed and embraced the best talent in the world in every field. The best physicists, mathematicians and engineers made America their home. Breakthroughs in fundamental research were soon commercialized by a new breed of entrepreneurs who demonstrated a terrific acumen for spotting their potential. Bell Labs could boast of nine Nobel laureates, including Clinton Davisson, who demonstrated something as fundamental as the wave nature of particles! America rapidly emerged as the land of equal opportunities, the likes of which had never been seen before. Tolerance, diversity, inclusion and meritocracy in their most idyllic form slowly cemented America's position as the most alluring destination for talent of all kind.

The American dream and its philosophy of business over everything else is further validated in the research by the New American Economy (NEA), a bipartisan research and advocacy organization in the US championing smart immigration policies that can create jobs for Americans. Immigrant entrepreneurs have long been an important part of America's economic success story. Some of the largest and most recognizable American companies were founded by immigrants or the children of immigrants, including household names such as Apple and Costco, as well as newcomers to the Fortune 500 list like Broadcom and Intuit. Even Levi's was created by two immigrants, Levi Strauss from Germany and Jacob Davis from Latvia, who invented the iconic staple of the American wardrobe—blue jeans.

Europe was fast losing its sheen and edge. Cambridge and Oxford had given way to MIT and Princeton. The next wave of global corporate powerhouses would emerge from the US. And every wave of successful enterprises would assist the scaling journey of the next wave of enterprises by strengthening the infrastructure of technology, talent and management know-how, thus making it easier for every successive generation of companies to attain scale. When IBM, GE, Westinghouse, Exxon, among others, peaked and subsequently lost steam, they were replaced by Microsoft, Oracle and Intel. When Microsoft, Oracle and Intel had outlived their glorious days, the mantle of innovation and growth fell on companies like Apple, Google, Facebook, and Amazon. America had apparently cracked the recipe for innovation and entrepreneurship.

With the advent of the Internet, the epicentre of innovation and entrepreneurship shifted to the Bay Area of California. The Internet spawned a new generation of start-ups.

The result of being the global leader of innovation is that the whole world becomes a market for your goods and services. Prosperity also creates an affluent domestic consumer base with sufficient discretionary income to test new ideas, products and services.

Post WWII, the US emerged as the undisputed leader of innovation, entrepreneurship and scaling. Japan and, to a much lesser degree, the Asian Tigers of Hong Kong, Taiwan, Singapore and South Korea got their act together, and for a few decades posed a real threat to the US. However, they could never develop the depth and multidimensionality of the US, and somewhere along the way all of them lost the plot and went down the path of Europe—growing old, tired, contented and harking back to past glory.

Chindia: The China–India Story

The year 1978 was a landmark for both China and India. While China embarked on a journey of aggressive and sustained reforms, India experimented with a coalition government for the first time in the history of independent India. The coalition government was a ragtag outfit cobbled together on an anti-Congress platform and had swept the elections in the previous year. The Janata Party was at the head of this coalition with Morarji Desai as the prime minister. Interestingly, the experiment with a coalition government didn't last for more than a couple of years and the nation re-elected the same leader that it had toppled with such vengeance just two years earlier. India's tryst with coalition governments continued in subsequent decades, and this reflected the complex and multidimensional polity of a nation torn by internal pulls and pressures on multiple dimensions.

In 1978, China also implemented a one-child policy. At this time, the fertility rate in China was 2.9, which was India's fertility rate in 2006! Sustained implementation of the one-child policy resulted in two things: a) China grew old before they got rich; b) it quickly translated to a significant increase in women's participation in the workforce. In contrast, India continued to remain youthful but with very low women's participation in the workforce because of persistent high childcare needs at home. Catalyst.Org, in a research report titled 'Women in the Workforce—India and China: Quick Take', reported that in 2018, women comprised just 23.6 per cent of the workforce in India despite constituting nearly 48 per cent of the population. In contrast, when it came to China, the imbalance was insignificant and in 2019 women comprised 43.7 per cent of the workforce and 48.7 per cent of the population.

India continued down the socialist path until 1991 when a catastrophic failure of centralized planning, with some push from the International Monetary Fund (IMF), forced economic reforms. India's reform process, initiated in 1991, was at best a half-hearted attempt and more a response to an existential crisis than a well-directed effort to lift the nation out of the low-growth regime (pejoratively referred to as the 'Hindu rate of growth') and place it on a higher trajectory. The lack of vision, the diversity of stakeholders, coupled with a democratic and federal structure, did not allow the reforms process to be rolled out with the same speed as in China. Decision-making by consensus slowed progress, and for every two steps forward there was a step backwards. As a result, by 2018, the gap between China and India widened significantly. In a report titled 'Comparing China and India by Economy', Stasticstimes. com presented that in 1978 the GDPs of China and India were $149 billion and $137 billion respectively, nearly the same. However, by 2018, the gap had widened significantly and the GDPs of these two nations were $13,608 billion and $2726 respectively. China's GDP was nearly five times that of India's.

China's Ability to Scale Shocked the World

China had been very suspicious of Western intent after a series of brushes with its powers in the nineteenth century that ended in defeat and resulted in the signing of humiliating treaties with Britain and other Western countries. These treaties gave Western traders and merchants the freedom to ignore Chinese laws and conduct business on unequal terms. Britain even fought two wars with China for the right to sell opium! And the Treaty of Nanking at the end of the wars allowed Britain to sell opium in China.

After a series of internal battles, the communists under Mao Zedong came to power in 1949. China's past experiences led it to stay away from any kind of Western influence. China grew insular with a vengeance. The Chinese were a determined race and every action of theirs since 1949 was motivated by a deep desire to revive their past glory, reclaim lost territory and undo past slights—real and imaginary. This included the burning desire to build a modern infrastructure and industry that had given the West the edge in the earlier decades. The Chinese had understood that to beat the West, they had to use Western methods, frameworks and structures.

In 1978, under Deng Xiaoping's leadership, China had aggressively driven economic reforms and opted for an 'export-led' growth model. Exports, and not domestic consumption, drove economic growth in the initial stages. Capital market reforms led to the creation of fully functional securities markets. The Shanghai stock exchange, opened in 1991, is today the fifth largest in the world in terms of the market capitalization of the stocks listed on the exchange.

On the back of Chinese protectionism and proclivity for creating Western-style infrastructure, the last two decades saw an epic rise of local consumer Internet companies that would rival their American equivalents. The constraints that smaller exporters in China faced were the discoverability of their products, logistics support and payments. Jack Ma spotted this opportunity in 1999 and set up Alibaba around these three vital needs of a rising China. Similarly, start-ups like JD.com, Baidu, Tencent, Didi and others took full advantage of a rising middle class and a friendly government and raced away to remarkable success, evoking both envy and adulation across the world.

These Chinese companies scaled to the level of their American equivalents in much shorter time frames, and the rapidity with which they attained such scale has been unprecedented. This held both investors and observers in awe. These start-ups in many ways mirrored China's rise as an economic superpower.

What Were the Factors that Contributed to This?

Geoffrey West, a British theoretical physicist who has done pioneering work in the area of growth, innovation and sustainability organizations, organisms and cities, points out that start-ups in China scaled at the same pace as American start-ups even though the Chinese market is very nascent in comparison. He further concludes that the only logical and uncomplicated inference is that in a vigorous fast-track setting, competitive free-market dynamics are sufficiently potent for systematic trends to emerge relatively quickly.

To this, we would like to add that China has imbibed some of the components of the great American dream, namely, a deep desire to excel and be the best in the world in anything they do. This reflects in the investments they have been making in science and technology, including weaponry and space exploration. They have looked at everything on a mind-blowing scale, including creating human capital capabilities. China now wins more medals in the Olympics than most other countries. However, China is different from the US on many other dimensions, including an ability to assimilate talent and culture from the rest of the world. Reid Hoffman points out in his book *Blitzscaling* that Didi Chuxing does 20 million rides per day in China, which is three times what Uber does worldwide. Similarly, the volume of mobile payments in China is nearly seventy-seven times that of the US in dollar terms. If not anything else, these are some very good indicators of the extent to which China, and Chinese start-ups and scale-ups, could dominate the world economy in the decades to come. Whether they actually do would depend to a large extent on how China deals with the rest of the world in its quest for superpower status.

Early global investors—such as Goldman Sachs, SoftBank and Tiger Global—in some of the Chinese start-ups reaped astronomical returns. A case in point was Yahoo!'s investment in Alibaba. When the American technology giant invested in Alibaba in 2005, little did it realize that the value of its investment of about $1 billion would be nearly $9.4 billion when Alibaba would list in 2014. The value of Yahoo!'s core business, when it was eventually sold to Verizon in 2017, was a paltry $4.48 billion in comparison.

India Emerges Reluctantly

Post liberalization in 1991, India enjoyed growth rates in the high single digits for several years. Its first-generation entrepreneurs emerged to take advantage of the labour arbitrage between the West and India. Y2K was a chance blessing and India's fetish for English education proved to be a boon. Outsourcing of information technology (IT) and business processes was a tidal wave that helped drive a hitherto unseen level of prosperity for the participants in this new industry. Many of the start-ups quickly scaled to become multibillion-dollar businesses. Outsourcing was a tide that lifted many ships. In economics, supply follows demand, though there are exceptions where a supply can create its own demand. The outsourcing industry in India soon faced a shortage of talent, but soon engineering and finishing schools sprung up to address this shortfall and remedy the situation. The success story of the outsourcing industry gave India a new swagger on the world stage.

The early success of IT outsourcing created a stampede to outsource. Very soon, every American company was rushing into India, some to find outsourcing vendors and others to set up their own captive centres. Their hope and belief was that every engineer in India would be like the IIT engineers they had seen in their own companies abroad.

However, very soon, the harsh realization dawned that less than a quarter of the engineers in India would have qualified for employment by their standards, leave alone do cutting-edge work at companies like Google. While this realization forced these companies to recalibrate at several levels, it did not distract from the basic thesis that a lot of work could be performed in India at much lower costs.

India's infrastructure was a shock to many American executives who were travelling to the country for the first time to evaluate outsourcing opportunities. It took many of them a while to digest the dichotomy of a nation which had such formidable prowess in software but a decaying and ramshackle physical infrastructure. In those days, even the airports in India were rickety and overcrowded small buildings. That has changed a bit now but once you step out of the airport, the story is not very different.

We recall an incident when a large and conservative American bank was considering outsourcing its 'collections' process to India. This was their first attempt at outsourcing. They were meeting several potential partners. At Daksh (where Sanjeev Aggarwal, the co-author of this book, was a founder) we were making a pitch in the boardroom. The entire mortgages management team of the bank was present. In the middle of the presentation, there was a power outage and in an instant there was a switchover from the grid to a diesel generator (DG). For all of us Indians in the room, who were used to power outages that lasted hours at a stretch, this ability to switch to a DG in a flash was the gold standard. Not so for the American bank executives in the room that day. They were in a bit of a shock when they realized power outages were common and a DG back-up was the norm. They took a while to digest this. The point is that the infrastructure in India was too creaky to depend upon. Private companies ended up creating a parallel infrastructure that not only increased costs but also impacted project timelines and the ability to scale rapidly. Same was the case with public transport as well. Companies that required employees to start their shifts at specific times with no leeway (like those that handled customer service) had to make arrangements to ferry employees from their homes to office and back. Some of these companies virtually ran transport services that would rival public transport organizations.

The Previous Decade Was the High Point for India

After the initial euphoria of the outsourcing boom, questions began being asked as to whether Indian entrepreneurs would ever attempt to solve India's problems and whether these problems could be solved profitably at all. The last ten years has answered this question pretty unequivocally.

India was to witness a tectonic shift in the overall start-up ecosystem. Indian entrepreneurs began going after the country's problems with a single-minded sense of purpose never seen before. This can be partly attributed to the availability of bold venture funding and the coming of age of the ecosystem. The venture capital industry in India has evolved and matured significantly since the turn of the century. Successive governments, through a combination of pragmatic policymaking and focused execution, have accelerated this journey.

The high point came when India earned the tag of the world's fastest growing large economy in 2016. Demonetization in November 2016 temporarily displaced India from its pole position, but the fact remained that it was the new land of opportunities. It was because of this sudden realization, along with some lost opportunities in China, that global VC firms made a beeline for India. This also kicked off a frenzy of entrepreneurial and VC activity.

Investing in India's growth story and macroeconomic potential became the new investment thesis!

For those familiar with the excesses of a previous era, some of the mistakes of this era seemed familiar. But as they say, every generation is entitled to learning their own lessons from scratch. Why learn from others' mistakes! In this latest wave of VC investing, the scenario hasn't been very different. After the initial blind rush, VCs soon figured out several things. First of all, India was not China. The depth of the market was not comparable. While the size of the populations were comparable—and by absolute standards India's GDP was already high and set to surge ahead rapidly—China's GDP was five times that of India's. Internet penetration as well as willingness to transact on the net was significantly lower in India. The multitude of languages added to the difficulties in creating market participation and penetration. The infrastructure was creaky. In a throwback to an earlier era when investors and companies outsourcing services were appalled by the infrastructure and the frequent power outages, newly arrived VCs too realized soon enough that the building blocks and infrastructure that could accelerate the scaling of new ideas were absent.

However, like the multinationals before them, VCs too recalibrated but this did not distract from the basic thesis that India was the next big opportunity, one they could not afford to miss. They learnt that patience, customization to Indian tastes and getting the price points right were critical.

When it came to a user base, the Indian online consumer market was grossly over-estimated and migration from offline to online was a slow process. Despite the size of the population and Internet penetration, online commerce did not take off as well as was expected. Anirban Sen, in an article in *Livemint* titled 'Amazon, Flipkart Power

New User Base in E-commerce in India', on 20 December 2018, wrote, based on an interview with the Flipkart CEO Kalyan Krishnamurthy, that Flipkart had around 16 million monthly active users in 2018. It was common knowledge that Amazon and Flipkart were running neck and neck, and hence the total number for both was between 30 and 35 million. Rashesh Shah, founder-CEO of Edelweiss, believes that unlike the US or China, the Indian market is subscale. The size of any market segment is relatively small. Therefore, to get to scale, start-ups need to evolve into conglomerate structures as they grow or expand into adjacencies either in terms of product or in terms of geography. Ola and Oyo have expanded into new geographies to stay on the growth path. On the contrary, Reliance Industries' growth aspirations have been met through a conglomerate structure with high diversification. Making unit economics work at subscale is particularly important in India. It makes it easier to scale and tap into adjacencies without the fear of running out of capital. Some start-ups in India, especially those in the consumer Internet space, have delayed optimizing their unit economics through liberal capital infusion. In India, M&A exits have not been easy. The buyers in any M&A are usually large companies which wish to accelerate their journeys by acquiring start-ups that have been at the cutting-edge of innovation in relevant domains. And there have not been enough large domestic companies in India that have the appetite for growing through acquisitions. As a result, most of the large M&A activity in India continues to be driven by American multinationals.

Achieving scale would therefore be a long-drawn-out journey. Deep-pocketed investors have been driving their portfolio companies to create scale rapidly through discounts and cashbacks. Soon enough, discounting as a way of accelerating growth began to face the wrath of regulators. For instance, as per the definition of a marketplace model, a marketplace was not allowed to influence pricing, and the regulators began coming down hard on it.

While we were putting together this story, we realized once again that this industry is grossly under-researched. While this is partially the case in more mature markets as well, when it comes to India, even the data—irrespective of the source—is spotty, inconsistent and unreliable. Therefore, multiple levels of validation are essential to reach any conclusion or to identify a trend.

The Fear of Missing Out!

Somewhere around 2014, VCs began demonstrating an appetite for much bigger ticket sizes and were willing to cut short the due diligence process. Hedge funds like Tiger Global changed the investing game with quick bold bets on audacious ideas. India's macroeconomic potential had caught the imagination of investors from across the world. Those who had tasted success in China as well as those who were too late to the party there rushed into India. The associated frenzy gave new meaning to the phrase 'fear of missing out (FOMO)'.

At its peak, FOMO manifested itself in two bad habits that VCs continued to demonstrate for some time. The first was 'herd mentality'. It was not at all surprising to find waves of similar ideas where one VC would back a particular start-up and a different VC would back an almost identical competitor. Ideas were in favour or out of favour based on what had worked in more mature markets. There was a new flavour every now and then. At one time, it was horizontal e-commerce start-ups, at a different point it was food tech and at yet another point it was fintech. Interestingly, when investors referred to food tech, it was never about food technology. It was almost always about 'delivering' food! The second bad habit was to back ideas that had succeeded in the West. Not enough thought was given to the context and the need for making relevant tweaks.

For instance, Rocket Internet's entire premise in India was built around such copycat ideas from a different geography, eventually resulting in their shutting shop and exiting from India in 2016. The frenzy to race ahead saw them make two fundamental compromises. Firstly, there were alleged ethics issues in many of the companies they backed. Ethics is always too fundamental to be compromised. Secondly, while imitation is a good form of flattery, it can't be the basis for building great companies.

Some years down the line, things were changing rapidly, almost as if an invisible tipping point had been breached. Two building blocks for scale took shape: the payments infrastructure and a unique citizen identity. These would drive innovation in a variety of industries, primarily in fintech. Reliance Jio proved to India and the rest of the world that innovation and disruption are not the prerogatives of twenty-five-year-olds. Large corporations led by leaders with imagination can disrupt and scale like the wind. India Stack, for instance, is demonstrating how a loose network of passionate professionals in India is replicating what Open Source, triggered twenty years ago in Palo Alto, achieved for software applications.

There is also the matter of (perceived) bias. One debate that refuses to die down is the 'bias' that investors tend to have for entrepreneurs with an IIT or IIM education. We don't have an opinion on this because everyone has a different story to tell. All we would say is that as human beings, we are inherently drawn to people like ourselves—people with similar backgrounds and sensibilities. And so, while it is true that a large chunk of the early investments in India went to such entrepreneurs, we would attribute this to the fact that the investing community drew heavily from people with these backgrounds. So, in some ways it was an old boys' network at play.

Our personal experience has been that entrepreneurship is going down the same path as cricket—drawn from elite backgrounds to start with but rapidly permeating to Tier 2 and 3 towns. India's best cricketers today come from modest backgrounds from smaller cities and towns. The best and most grounded entrepreneurs too come from similar backgrounds and not necessarily with an Ivy League education. We have no doubt that we will see many more of these entrepreneurs in the years to come, and their ideas and execution will power India's journey forward.

Flipkart's Founding and Exit Were Big Turning Points

While InMobi emerged as India's first unicorn, Flipkart stole the imagination of the Indian public for two reasons: a) it was a consumer brand; and b) it became India's answer to Amazon. For a long time, it was believed that

India's Google would be Google, India's Facebook would be Facebook and India's Amazon would be Amazon. But no, India's Amazon was Flipkart!

From February 2018, the market was abuzz with rumours about Flipkart's imminent acquisition by Walmart. There was also a rumour about a late wild-card entry by Amazon. Knowing how fickle Amazon had been in the past when it came to M&A, nobody took this seriously, though several reliable sources reported that Amazon had officially put in a bid to purchase 60 per cent of Flipkart around the time Walmart was reportedly in the final stages of acquiring a large stake. Apparently, the offer was on a par with Walmart's. In addition, Amazon was offering Flipkart a $2 billion break-up fee in case the Walmart deal fell apart as a result of Flipkart's prenuptial flirtation with a rival contender. None of this can ever be verified but the market buzz on this, including specifics, was consistent across sources.

The sentiment at Flipkart, however, was pro-Walmart for several reasons, not least of which was the adverse view that the Competition Commission of India (CCI) could potentially take of an Amazon–Flipkart combine. In a nutshell, Amazon had dragged its feet like it had done before on other deals in India. It was simply a matter of too little too late.

On 9 May 2018, the suspense finally ended. Walmart and Flipkart entered into a definitive agreement where Walmart would buy a 77 per cent stake in Flipkart for $16 billion, valuing the company at a whopping $20.8 billion. Walmart was paying a hefty premium for a late entry. They could have potentially acquired a controlling stake much earlier but had missed the bus. The management presentation to employees went viral on WhatsApp. The highlight of the deck wasn't the value of the deal; it was that co-founder Sachin Bansal did not have a role to play in Flipkart's new avatar.

Over the last couple of years, there had been increasing doubt about the Indian start-up market being able to provide its investors successful exits. This single transaction provided everyone with some much-needed reassurance, at least for now.

When Sachin and Binny Bansal started Flipkart sometime in October 2007, little did they realize that they had unknowingly triggered an avalanche. Their success story ignited a new wave of entrepreneurship that led to a deluge of first-generation entrepreneurs. Suddenly, VC money was easily available for entrepreneurs with big ideas. At one point of time, the tables were turned and venture capitalists were literally pitching to entrepreneurs; or if that seems a bit of an exaggeration, then at least entrepreneurs could pick and choose from among multiple term sheets.

Big Bets and the Valuation Game

'Disruption', 'network effect', 'winner takes all' were all the new buzzwords and phrases. Valuations were more about demand–supply dynamics and scarcity value than any fundamentals.

Wild swings in valuation became the norm as the game evolved within a sector. When Jabong was finally acquired by Flipkart in July 2016 for a paltry $70 million, one could not help wonder how things could have gone downhill so quickly from the winter of 2014 when a potential deal with Amazon fell through because the asking price of $1.2 billion was a bit too steep.

The story was to repeat with Snapdeal and a host of other consumer Internet companies. This had happened before with Yahoo! in the US, and this was happening now in India. These new businesses had all been scaled around an unconventional business model. The elements of this brave new model were: a) burn money and change consumer behaviour; b) race ahead of the competition by acquiring deep-pocketed investors; c) stay ahead of the pack and use the network effect to take away market share from competition; and d) kill the competition by bleeding them to death by offering steep discounts.

The last man standing would be the winner in this model. It was a risky game, and there were several uncertainties. One never knew how long and how many million dollars it would take to be the last man standing. What's more, there was no guarantee that the market would be one where the winner would take all. And, even if you were the last man standing, there was no guarantee of an exit, via a strategic buyout or an initial public offering (IPO). This was another fear (that Indian start-ups could not attract large strategic buyouts) that the Flipkart–Walmart deal dispelled to some extent, besides proving the point that VCs who made big, bold bets in India could see exits.

New VCs and Young Founders Come of Age

Founder–VC tussles are not uncommon. In India too, some founders were not able to scale and lead their start-ups after they crossed certain tipping points and had to be replaced. Some of these changes were amicable, others more acrimonious. Zivame, Housing, Flipkart and a few others saw board-led management changes at the top. Some very promising start-ups also came apart because governance issues were swept under the carpet.

However, what stands out is that most young founders and their young management teams demonstrated an amazing ability to scale as fast as their start-ups, fuelling the counter-intuitive view that experience is often overplayed!

It wasn't long before founders like Sachin and Binny Bansal, Vijay Shekhar Sharma (Paytm), Ritesh Aggarwal (Oyo), Bhavish Aggarwal (Ola) and several others attained global fame and iconic status.

The Flipkart and TaxiForSure Mafias

What do Tesla Motors, LinkedIn, Palantir Technologies, SpaceX, Airbnb, YouTube, Yelp and Yammer have in common? When eBay acquired PayPal, most of the founding team of the company quit and went their own ways to start again, and have since been collectively referred to as the PayPal mafia. Peter Thiel, founder and CEO of PayPal, was the de facto don of this mafia! Elon Musk (Tesla, SpaceX, Solar City, Hyperloop and others), Reid Hoffman (LinkedIn) and Luke Nosek (Founders Fund, Gigafund) are all part of this mafia. It is difficult to fathom how such a bunch of talented rock stars were once part of a single start-up.

In India, Flipkart and TaxiForSure became academies for entrepreneurship, and employees at these start-ups quit at different points of time to start on their own. They were not only encouraged by the founders of the companies they were quitting, but were even funded by them.

These founders had a strange capacity to inspire very ordinary people to attempt the extraordinary. More than 200 start-ups emerged from the Flipkart and TaxiForSure stables, and more than half of those are still active and on to something. (TaxiForSure was acquired by its larger rival Ola in March 2015 for $200 million and the brand was shut down eighteen months later.)

People were giving up careers in well-established companies and taking the plunge. This was another sign that entrepreneurship was slowly becoming something to be proud of. On campuses, start-ups enjoy Day 0 and Day 1 slots. Most educational institutions now have entrepreneurship cells, and students have begun pursuing it even before they graduate. Not surprisingly, the IITs and IIMs, home to some of the earliest campus accelerators in the country, have an encouraging number of promising start-ups. Ather Energy, the maker of India's first electric scooter, was incubated at IIT Madras, as was Uniphore, which makes speech-based mobility solutions. IIT Bombay, meanwhile, has incubated cyber security solutions provider Lucideus Tech, DIY drone provider Drona Aviation and energy-saving fan-maker Atomberg, among others. The list is quite long.

When Sachin and Binny Bansal took the leap, few realized that they would create a permanent line that would divide the history of modern entrepreneurship in India in two: 'before' and 'after' Flipkart!

In Conclusion

India's scaling journey has been different from both that of the US as well as China. India is a large and growing market. Scaling is relatively in its infancy compared to the other two countries but the country is growing up fast. In some areas like telecom and payments, India has leapfrogged ahead. Physical infrastructure is likely to be a sore point for decades to come. We don't know if this is a problem that India can ever solve completely because of too many contradictions, conflicts, poverty and a democratic federal structure. The unintended consequence of this is that the excessive friction on the ground gives an edge to local entrepreneurs who understand the dynamics deeply as opposed to multinational corporations. Therefore, while India may never be able to produce a Google, it can very well produce a Flipkart. And the reason is straightforward. Any business that encounters friction on the ground is normally better understood by local entrepreneurs. In the Western world, both public and private infrastructures are evolved and efficient. Therefore, building a business that depends on external capabilities is unlikely to create challenges in delivering consistent customer experience. In India, full-stack models tend to work better. A full-stack model is about owning the supply chain or at least being able to exercise a significant control over the key components. Scaling therefore isn't as easy as it would have been if a business did not have to create the whole supply chain. Local entrepreneurs understand this intuitively and quickly.

However, India's entrepreneurs have clearly emerged as among the best in the world, and the ideas they are working on are extremely ambitious. Their tenacity and talent need to be seen and appreciated in the light of their constant uphill battle against a not-too-friendly climate for business. In the next few decades, we are hopeful of seeing many more 'unicorns'—real 'unicorns'—that are profitable, sustainable and solve real problems.

4

Organization DNA

We believe that it's really important to come up with core values that you can commit to. And by commit, we mean that you're willing to hire and fire based on them. If you're willing to do that, then you're well on your way to building a company culture that is in line with the brand you want to build.

—Tony Hsieh, CEO, Zappos

On 19 February 2017, Susan Fowler, a software engineer at Uber, wrote a blog post in which she described in detail the sexual harassment she had to suffer at the workplace. In the post, she recounted how the company's human resources refused to punish her former manager, who had propositioned her. She also described other gory details about the prevailing toxic culture in the company. Silicon Valley was revered by the rest of the world as an innovation factory. However, the many skeletons in the cupboard, including the widely prevalent 'bro culture', was a well-kept secret. This blog post spilled the muck into the open.

Sarah Benstead, in an article titled 'Bro Culture and Why It's an Issue for Startups' published on 18 October 2018 on breathehr.com, describes a 'bro culture' as one that prioritizes young macho men with obnoxious and toxic behaviour above all others. The average 'bro' tends to be a hustling guy who places winning and success above respect for others. 'Bros' operate in an environment of excessive partying and bullying, with harassment of colleagues being the everyday norm. She goes on to say that typically start-ups with a 'bro culture' encourage excessive partying as a motivating tool and the office is generally a toxic pot of gossip and negative chatter. This is not unique to the Western world. Several young start-ups in India too have been accused of a bro culture. Many women have told us that they have not felt comfortable in a culture where a bunch of aggressive alpha males take important decisions outside of office hours during late-night beer bashes. Women often find it difficult to participate in these decision-making forums because of safety issues or because they have children to look after at home. Some women cope by outwardly trying to be a part of this culture, but it begins to take a toll.

Psychologists believe that 'bros' can be good at hustling, breaking the rules and driving outcomes without a care for the means. Since most start-ups aim to scale rapidly and quickly hit the proverbial jackpot, they tend to nurture the bro culture or at least turn a blind eye to it. Often, this can get you some quick wins, and for the outside world, without any knowledge of the inner workings, this start-up can come across as the paragon of corporate excellence, a conqueror. Until someone like Susan Fowler chooses to break the silence or an innocent child in the crowd blurts out that the emperor is wearing nothing at all, and the cry is then taken up by others.

Following the uproar in the aftermath of the blog post, the mercurial founder-CEO of Uber, Travis Kalanick, was eventually fired. There was some more collateral damage and a few more heads rolled. Tech investors Dave McClure and Justin Caldbeck were a few of them.

In the months that followed, many more similar stories surfaced, including the widespread gender pay gap in the technology industry. In the same article, Sarah Benstead also pointed out that Loretta Lee, a former Google employee, said she was subjected to 'lewd comments, pranks and even physical violence' on a daily basis between 2008 and 2016. It was a 'Me Too' moment all over again! Susan Fowler was the catalyst the women in Silicon Valley had been waiting for.

In January 2016, the Indian prime minister, Narendra Modi, unveiled the Stand-up India scheme in front of a large gathering of the start-up community. Sitting beside him were two entrepreneurs admired across the globe— Adam Neumann and Travis Kalanick. In a little over three years, these two had gone from being lionized to living in disgrace. Another entrepreneur, whose start-up had become a unicorn just a couple of weeks earlier, also spoke on the occasion and referred to the newly acquired 'unicorn' tag five times in the speech. This start-up no longer exists. Life has a way of reminding us that fame and glory can be really short-lived. Marilyn Monroe had once said, 'Fame will go by and, so long, I've had you, fame. If it goes by, I've always known it was fickle.

So at least it's something I experience, but that's not where I live.'

Strangely, or not so strangely, the investors in both WeWork and Uber were the same, Benchmark Capital and SoftBank. VC and PE (private equity) firms, especially those that come in late at the growth stage, often push very hard and tend to turn a blind eye to anything that can slow down growth in the short term. By the time these late-stage VC/PE firms make their entry, all the early investors are either exiting with big profits or sitting on huge unrealized gains. Therefore, these investors tend to be more impatient when it comes to seeing their investment grow. They obviously bank on the hope that growth, even if unnatural or detrimental, would hide the scum it generates. Uber was struggling with an inflated valuation that was set to rights by the public market, and WeWork, for all practical purposes, came down like a pack of cards despite SoftBank throwing good money after bad. After Kalanick's ignominious exit and Dara Khosrowshahi's infamous 'MIT Equals Mathematically Incompetent Theories' tweet in 2018, Uber is now trying to enter the fintech space!

In the rise and fall of these two companies is a lesson for start-ups and investors.

At a start-up, culture equals founder/s. Period. Unfortunately, a simple question of self-awareness has been complicated by too much that is going around on culture. This tends to be lapped up by those who are yet to have life experiences that could have shaped their view of who they are and what they stand for. In the absence of these life experiences that help crystallize self-awareness, culture is just a fuzzy concept that can sometimes be confused for office décor or espoused values. It is neither.

Starting with the Key Takeaways about Culture

- Culture manifests itself at three levels: a) at the level of artefacts like office décor and dress codes; b) at the level of espoused values like 'customer centricity', 'speed and agility', etc.; and c) the tacit stuff around who gets rewarded or what gets rewarded. The first is the least representative of culture. Espoused values are a statement of intent rather than reality. Only the last one is the true representation of it.
- Culture is difficult to build and shape. Once it has taken shape, it is even more difficult to change.
- Culture can be driven both through a broad set of principles and through a detailed document or a combination of the two.
- Culture can be bottom-up as well as top-down depending on the circumstances.
- While some cultures can be out-and-out toxic and detrimental, there are otherwise no good or bad cultures.
- There is a conceptually simple playbook for ensuring that culture is embedded deeply in an organization, but its execution is not as simple.
- There is a simple set of principles for transporting the core culture of a company to new locations as it expands.

Culture Is the Invisible Hand

Adam Smith, the Scottish thinker and one of the early economists, introduced a metaphor for the invisible hand in his book *The Wealth of Nations*. The metaphor lucidly explains the unobservable market forces that move the free market economy and how this helps the demand and supply of goods to reach equilibrium automatically without any form of centralized coordination. Through individual self-interest and freedom of production as well as consumption, the best interests of society as a whole are fulfilled. The constant interplay of individual pressures on market supply and demand causes the natural movement of prices and the flow of trade.

Each free exchange creates signals about which goods and services are valuable and how difficult they are to bring to the market. These signals, captured in the price system, spontaneously direct competing consumers, producers, distributors and intermediaries—each pursuing their individual plans—to fulfil the needs and desires of others.

This is a perfect analogy for organization culture— the invisible hand that quietly guides the actions of all the employees in the company. Each interaction creates signals about which behaviours and actions are acceptable and which are not. Just as the price system spontaneously drives individual action in a free market, the reward and penalty system drives behaviours in a company. The rewards need not be monetary. They could be as simple as acknowledgement, or just a word of thanks. They could also be about who is promoted and who is not. The penalties could be as simple as a hard stare and reprimand or as important as a decision to not promote someone to a leadership role. Just as a free market works more efficiently than a centrally planned economy, a company with a well-communicated and well-executed culture could work with far more agility and coordination than a company driven entirely by written policies.

Some Cultures Trigger Strong Reactions

There have been multiple headlines in recent years about Amazon's grinding work culture. People lined up on both sides of the debate. Every iconic company tends to consciously or unconsciously create some kind of a cult around its work culture. In the *New York Times* dated 15 August 2015, there was an article titled, 'Inside Amazon: Wrestling Big Ideas in a Bruising Workplace' by Jodi Kantor and David Streitfield. In this article, the authors claimed that 'workers are encouraged to tear apart one another's ideas in meetings, toil long and late (emails arrive past midnight, followed by text messages asking why they were not answered), and held to standards that the company boasts are "unreasonably high" . . . Losers leave or are fired in annual culling of the staff— "purposeful Darwinism," one former Amazon human resources director said. Some workers who suffered from cancer, miscarriages and other personal crises said they had been evaluated unfairly or edged out rather than given time to recover.'

'On the flipside', the authors of the piece also discovered that 'more than 100 current and former Amazonians— members of the leadership team, human resources executives, marketers, retail specialists and engineers who worked on projects from the Kindle to grocery delivery to the recent mobile phone launch—described how they tried to reconcile some of the punishing aspects of their workplace with what many called its thrilling power to create . . . In interviews, some said they thrived at Amazon precisely because it pushed them past what they thought were their limits. Many employees are motivated by thinking big and knowing that we haven't scratched the surface on what's out there to invent'.

Susan Harker, whose current LinkedIn profile shows that she was the vice president for talent acquisition at Amazon in 2017, is quoted in the same article as saying, 'This is a company that strives to do really big, innovative, groundbreaking things, and those things aren't easy. When you're shooting for the moon, the nature of the work is really challenging. For some people it doesn't work.'

Therefore, while some saw the work culture as harsh, others found it energizing.

Cultures come in different hues and shades. Depending upon what defines a company and gives it the edge, some have a strong tech culture while others have a very strong research and development culture. Some have a manufacturing/production culture while others have a marketing and/or sales culture. An M&A between a company with a strong tech culture and one with a strong sales culture, for instance, is very likely to have some serious issues around mutual respect and appreciation of what the other brings to the table. M&A integrations therefore need to be handled with a lot of sensitivity and understanding.

In addition to this layer of culture, which is correlated with the core capability of the firm, there are other dimensions around aggression, goal orientation, people orientation, collaboration, decision-making styles, etc. Aggressive cultures usually have low tolerance for not meeting outcomes while soft and collaborative cultures usually place a lot more emphasis on effort and context. An aggressive culture can come across as strong and a bit polarizing in the sense that one is either a great fit or an utter misfit. In such an organization, hiring and firing is quite clinical. Past contributions and loyalty often do not count for much. Changes in leadership are common and swift. Integrity issues are dealt with based on convenience, or they tend to take a black-and-white approach. A soft culture, on the other hand, accommodates a range of personalities where live and let live is the way of life. Even when an organization with such a culture looks at performance, it does not easily ignore the efforts that were put in, or the honesty and the loyalty of the individual being evaluated. It does not mean that an organization with this culture would never ask a person to leave. It would do so after a great deal of thought and serious consideration on humanitarian grounds. Integrity issues are dealt with based on the nature of the breach and the circumstances of the individual committing it. Neither culture is good or bad. An aggressive culture with a strong focus on results and accountability could potentially degenerate into becoming toxic, while a soft and accommodating culture could degenerate into complacency and poor performance. In our opinion, the culture at Amazon or Flipkart would qualify as being aggressive and that at IBM or BigBasket as soft.

Toxic cultures, on the other hand, tend to engender behaviours, right from the very top, bordering on what is commonly accepted as unethical and/or immoral. Companies with such cultures can survive for a while and even achieve iconic status when the going is good, but cracks invariably begin to show up sooner or later. All it takes is a disgruntled employee who becomes a whistle-blower. Clearly this culture is totally undesirable! It's only a matter of time before a company with such a culture is faced with public reckoning and put through purgatory from which it would either emerge in a different form or meet its end. Complacent cultures, on the other hand, can soon degenerate into employment guarantee programmes where poor performers can hide forever.

It's our gut feeling that aggressive start-ups tend to disrupt a little better, demonstrate impatience for results and can be a bit polarizing. On the other hand, start-ups with a soft culture tend to be a little more stable with a higher happiness index. There is certainly a bit of generalization in painting these cultures, and we advise you to take these as broad indicators, with a range of variations and exceptions. As we said earlier in the book, generalizations are helpful only to individuals who understand deeply the criticality of the context and the reality of exceptions.

Is Culture Change Possible?

This is a common question we encounter. Can we change our culture? Edgar Schein, the demigod of corporate culture, recounts a very interesting story (in his book *The Corporate Culture Survival Guide*") in the days preceding and following the launch of the IBM personal computer (PC). Digital Equipment Corporation (DEC) was an iconic Silicon Valley start-up built on the premise that their products were designed for the 'smart' user. To do this, they hired smart people and gave them total freedom. No one, including the CEO, Ken Olsen, could overrule them on ideas. DEC was doing terrific until IBM launched a PC for the 'dumb' user. DEC hadn't realized that most smart users would have actually preferred a product designed for the dumb user. When DEC had to respond, they could not reach a consensus on the features a product that would compete with the IBM PC needed to have. Their four engineering teams launched four different products, each with its own bells and whistles, which ultimately bombed at the marketplace. This was DEC's death knell, and it was ultimately acquired by Compaq.

The lesson in this is that a culture that made DEC a truly iconic company failed to work when it was time to create a product for the mass market. It required a culture of discipline, hierarchical working and structured decision-making while DEC had a highly empowering culture, and the company could not make the change. Culture change is not about flipping a switch. It is deeply reflective of who the company is if it were a person.

Therefore, while it is possible to tweak your culture a bit and sharpen some components, it is very difficult to make a large-scale change. For instance, if you love spending your time reading a book by yourself or having a drink with close friends, you can never really enjoy going out daily to meet and woo new people.

Is Culture a Top-down Thing or a Bottom-up Thing?

In 2002, Samuel Palmisano, an IBM veteran of thirty years, was appointed the CEO. In 2003, he initiated a company-wide project to review its values. The approach IBM took was to involve its entire global workforce in rediscovering what IBM stood for and the relevance of some of the values in the new competitive landscape. The belief was that nothing meaningful could be discovered or created without involving employees on the frontlines. Over the decades, IBM had evolved in terms of geographical spread, the products it built and customers it served, and hence the intent of this exercise was to also figure out if it needed to embrace some new values. Palmisano and his leadership team seeded some thoughts to kick-start the exercise.

It is difficult to draw a hasty conclusion that the success of IBM in the following decade was attributable to this exercise that helped rediscover its identity, though Palmisano cannot be faulted for giving a good bit of the credit to this bottom-up exercise.

In recent times, Dara Khosrowshahi initiated a similar exercise at Uber.

Our view is that a bottom-up exercise of this nature made a lot of sense in these two contexts. IBM had been around for more than eighty-five years when this exercise was initiated. During this period, the founder had exited and many professional CEOs had helmed the company. The identity of the company and the founding principles were lost to the employees somewhere along the line. Also, IBM had expanded its footprint and shuffled its portfolio of products and services significantly and some of the principles needed to be revisited. Uber, on the other hand, had gone through a massive upheaval and loss of morale. It was absolutely critical to get the employees to participate in an exercise designed to rediscover and reinforce the core of the company. Winning the trust and respect of employees at this crucial juncture was of paramount importance to Uber. It was a make-or-break situation. And there could be no better way of doing this than actively involving a majority of them in reframing what the company stood for.

In most other situations, in which more than 90 per cent of start-ups find themselves, we believe a top-down approach makes a lot more sense. We'll talk about this in a bit.

Culture Is the Invisible Stuff

Culture is always tacit and unstated. For example, you might notice that in a particular company disagreements are rare and there is seeming consensus at the end of meetings. It is tempting to believe that the culture is one of collaboration. But don't go by what is visible. Culture is always about peering under the surface and spotting what is unsaid. The consensus that you may see in this company could be false because the culture could be of outward compliance but inward resistance. This means that 'even though we may have agreed on something, I'll go back and do my own thing'! In a different company, conflict may be dealt with openly and alignment on expected actions could happen quickly.

Culture is about behaviours that are rewarded or punished. This is precisely the reason why in some companies people take cross-functional projects seriously while in some other companies they do not get the participation and commitment needed. This is because the first set of companies encourages and rewards good corporate citizens who go beyond their day job, whereas leaders in the second set of companies treat cross-functional projects as a diversion and don't encourage their team members to participate actively in them.

The reason why it is so difficult to reward the right behaviours and penalize the wrong ones is because very often the wrong behaviours produce short-term gains for an organization and the right behaviours short-term pain. We saw a few examples earlier.

As we illustrated with the example of DEC, it is not easy to change culture because it usually represents the DNA of the leadership team/founders, and individuals evolve very slowly. One may, therefore, legitimately ask: 'If organizations can't change who they are then what is the whole point of understanding culture?' It is the same thing as asking: 'If individuals can't fundamentally change who they are then what is the whole point of developing better self-awareness?' Self-awareness helps individuals better understand themselves in relation to the world around them, and hence deal with situations more effectively. The lesson in this is that you should know what your organization's culture is even if you can't change it easily. If you know consensus cannot be taken at face value in your organization, you can work to change it or evolve a workaround.

People often ask us this question: How should a start-up (or even a more mature company) drive its culture across the company?

We believe culture can be driven through a combination of storytelling and living it every day. While the latter is more important and far more difficult, the power of storytelling cannot be undermined. I saw Kris Canekeratne, founder and CEO of Virtusa Corporation, do this very well. To communicate the power of teamwork and the importance of a leader who accepts responsibility when things go wrong, he would recall how Michael Schumacher would always credit the team for his wins. Michael Schumacher is widely regarded as one of the greatest Formula One drivers ever. In stark contrast, when, after losing a race, another famous contemporary of Schumacher was asked why he didn't win that day, his response was, 'We didn't lose because of bad driving!' In the same vein, Canekeratne would also say that when things went well, leaders needed to give credit to the team, but when things didn't go as planned, they needed to look in the mirror and ask themselves what they could have done better. It's not easy to do this, and I think he got across this message wherever he went. The other, and more important, component of driving culture is about a critical mass of leaders living it every day. One of the most well understood elements of human psychology is that people learn to imitate the behaviours of those they admire and/or those who control their rewards. Therefore, any company, however big or small, can drive a practice, behaviour or value if the 5–15 senior-most leaders are collectively and strongly committed to it. Whether it is conducting meetings effectively, or demonstrating speed and a sense of urgency, respect for people, transparency or anything for that matter, it can be driven if these 5–15 leaders are serious about it. And the way it works is that these 5–15 individuals demonstrate and live what they want to drive every day and encourage the same strongly in their direct reports. Their direct reports will soon start living this value or behaviour. It will slowly percolate down and across. People evaluate the culture of a place by seeing how leaders behave. A hundred CEO speeches on culture are not as good as one demonstrated behaviour. So ensure that you use all opportunities to demonstrate the culture you wish to create. Ensure that ten of your colleagues do the same. There will be moments when you would want to take shortcuts. While they may be inevitable once in a while, be very careful about taking those that undermine the culture. Living the culture every day also means embedding the underlying values and culture components into the objectives and key results (OKRs) and performance management process. Decisions to promote individuals into leadership roles too need to be based on culture fit and alignment among other things. This needs to be widely communicated and understood.

For instance, at BigBasket, we have tried to drive 'a maniacal focus on customers' as well as 'a sense of speed and urgency in everything we do'. These have been called out and widely communicated. However, only the first of the two has taken root while the second one hasn't. The reason is that almost everyone in the leadership team lives and breathes 'customer focus' every day, whereas there is no deep and visible commitment to speed and urgency. This brings up an important point: no organization can ever get everything right. BigBasket is a classic case of getting a few things so correct that it could mask a few other weak links.

There are two reasons why it is so difficult to drive several good practices simultaneously across the breadth and depth of the company: a) getting the 5–15 individuals to agree and sign off with their heart and soul on many diverse things is not easy; and b) weak leaders are often reluctant to take ownership for driving behaviours and instead rely on peripheral and distracting fixes like compensation plans and organizational structure that they think would magically induce the right behaviours.

Broad Guidelines versus a Detailed Guide

The choice is between laying out a few broad guidelines and creating a detailed document. The commonly quoted example of each of the two approaches is Nordstrom and Netflix respectively.

In a different context, the British Constitution is unwritten, whereas the Indian and American Constitutions are documented in a fair amount of detail and have tried to address every possible scenario. These two constitutions have undergone a good number of amendments to address scenarios that could not have been anticipated when they were drafted. On a different note, we have all wondered at some point as to how a country like Britain, without a written constitution, could run for even a day! By all accounts it appears that an unwritten constitution hasn't handicapped Britain.

Nordstrom has a set of nine values like trust, respect, humility, loyalty and so on. The company and those who run it now (great-grandsons of the founder, Pete Nordstrom) believe that 'values define who we are, and if they change we become something else. Practices are ways of doing things that express our values. Practices may serve us well for long periods of time, but they're not values, and therefore can be changed without changing our culture'. Robert Spector is one of America's leading experts on customer experience and employee experience and has authored several business books. In 1995, in his bestselling book *The Nordstrom Way: Inside America's Number One Customer Service Company,* he described in great detail how Nordstrom created the culture they are known for. He says:

After all is said and done, the reason why Nordstrom stays relevant and competitive is that the company attracts people who share these core values. Retail is a relationship business, and no relationship—whether business or personal—can survive without trust, respect, loyalty, awareness, humility, communication and collaboration.

The culture at Nordstrom is not laid out in detail and employees are advised to ask their managers when in doubt.

In contrast, Netflix has a fairly detailed culture document with examples and illustrations. It was one of the most 'shared' documents on the Internet for a very long time.

Our own view is that the advice 'ask your manager when in doubt' can be helpful only if managers understand nuances of the culture reasonably well. We suspect that as organizations scale, most managers might end up being as befuddled as their team members, and can do little to answer questions on values and culture. These are not easy questions that can have black-and-white canned responses. They need a deeper and nuanced understanding. For example, terms like loyalty, trust and integrity are subtle and can be interpreted differently by different individuals. In the absence of illustrations and examples, they are not easy to understand and contextualize. Therefore, we believe it is important to: a) help leaders at senior and mid management to first of all really understand why culture even matters. Most leaders, brought up on the common diet of left-brained education and thinking, don't easily get it. They think it is some mumbo-jumbo soft stuff. But once they get it, they usually do a good job of using it well.

So do everything to help them get it. In companies we were associated with, we used game theory to get across culture to the left-brained individuals who dominate the start-up world. It is also important to: b) have a document that lays out the values and culture components with examples and illustrations, and use opportunities to communicate and reinforce these. For those who haven't heard of 'game theory', it is a theoretical framework for looking at different scenarios among competing players and producing optimal decisions. Using game theory has been very helpful in real-world scenarios for situations such as pricing competition, among others. Game theory is a powerful tool to explain a wide range of social behaviours.

Having said this, the obvious question is: Do companies known for creating iconic cultures not suffer from employee dissatisfaction? Of course they do. In an article in Business Insider, published on 17 February 2018, titled, 'I got a job at Nordstrom and discovered the "best company to work for" has a shark tank culture no one ever talks about', Aaron Valentic, who had worked at Nordstrom for three years, called out some of the very dysfunctional elements of the company's culture.

Culture is not important because it makes everyone love everything about the company. It is important because it is the invisible hand that guides the actions of the company. It is the intangible stuff that makes people want to work for you. Calling out culture and making it a part of your everyday life just helps you attract the kind of people who fit in well. And it helps the company move ahead with speed without leaders having to take the trouble of explaining the why of every action to everyone.

Culture Can Determine Your Talent Strategy

Though some would like to believe that there are universal approaches to attract and retain talent, the truth is that there is no one right way to define talent or attract and retain it.

Let us illustrate this statement with two real examples. Two companies we were both very closely associated with, namely, Daksh and BigBasket, had different business contexts and cultures that translated into very different lenses with which they viewed talent. Each approach was right in its own context. Daksh was India's leading business process outsourcing company that was acquired by IBM sometime in 2004. BigBasket is India's largest online grocery superstore and a unicorn.

Marshall Goldsmith, a well-known business educator and coach, wrote a well-acclaimed book titled *What Got You Here Won't Get You There* in 2007. The title itself is a very powerful quote in a specific context. The counter to this is that if you forget who you are, where you come from and what got you here, you certainly won't get anywhere. The true essence of the BigBasket story is that the founders never forgot the lessons from their last venture, Fabmart. There the founders realized that it was easy to spend money to build large and expensive teams, but not easy to run a business with thin margins profitably. Some of these lessons were etched deeply in their DNA and impacted the way they viewed talent.

The head of supply chain at BigBasket had started his career as an inventory controller. The product head started as a technology lead. The basic belief had always been to hire people (internally or laterally) who could punch above their weight. The corollary to this was that people who had faced challenges in performing at high standards were given support and coaching rather than being put through the wringer. Education pedigree was never an important screening parameter. Even individuals with great education had to pass a tough test of culture-fit, in which they had to work with those with less privileged education with humility.

Another belief has been that average people backed by strong processes can deliver outstanding results on scale. This translated to a strong emphasis on process and a recruitment philosophy where those in the field had to have strong execution skills but did not necessarily have to be astute problem-solvers or thinkers because the processes to support them were developed centrally. This helped optimize costs.

The innovation quotient at BigBasket was kept high through thoughtful acquisitions, which were seen more from the perspective of bringing on board young and energetic entrepreneurs who could keep the innovation engine firing. This was another interesting talent acquisition strategy.

However, some of this thinking that was based on past baggage resulted in some difficulty in differentiating good costs from bad costs. And this reflected in delays in bringing on board key hires, which, one could argue, slowed the growth journey a bit.

Daksh, in contrast, was a very profitable business. Sanjeev Aggarwal, one of the co-authors of this book, and co-founder and CEO, came from a background of building scale businesses and had learnt that when the opportunity ahead of you was large, you needed to be ready to capitalize on it quickly. The best way to do that, he believed, was to hire people who did not need supervision or guidance. So the folks in the business units were all terrific problem-solvers and the business heads were real CEOs who didn't give a damn about corporate functions if they couldn't solve their problems. Corporate functions didn't call the shots. Instead, they were seen as providing expertise and assistance in solving problems.

The culture was aggressive and non-performers were not given a place to hide for long.

Education pedigree was seen as a good surrogate for brain power and people were hired ahead of the curve. Leaders had to have good execution skills with an ability to think and communicate clearly. Assertiveness was an important trait because the basic belief was that it was the prerequisite for doing anything good. If you couldn't speak up or express yourself where it mattered, it was a sign of a cultural misfit.

The talent strategy that each of these two companies adopted was perfectly suited to its business context and culture. Each has been a big success story. However, each had its own downsides. Companies and people come wrapped in a package like a box of chocolates. The inability to understand and appreciate the business context and culture and how it shapes the talent strategy can be fatal.

Seeding Culture in a New Location or Country

Any journey of scale requires expansion into a new geography—it could be expanding into new areas within a country or it could be an international expansion. Airbnb, Grab, Uber, Oyo Rooms, Ola Cabs are some of the unicorns minted in this decade that have expanded internationally. Scores of unicorns of a previous era have successfully expanded to new geographies and the playbook is reasonably well-established. It is helpful to understand some of the principles of transporting the culture and good practices of a company that plans to expand nationally or internationally.

Get a leader who is a beacon of the company culture to be the head of the city or country into which your start-up is expanding. This is the most effective way to seed a new region. It is also important to select the early hires thoughtfully and screen for culture alignment carefully.

Intense and meaningful communication is critical, especially until things settle down and trust gets built. Communication should be a mix of electronic as well as physical travel. Never undermine the importance of frequent travel at this stage.

It is important to demonstrate cultural sensitivity when you expand your start-up to a totally different region or country.

Besides, some elementary management practices need to be well executed in a cross-cultural context, and as a business expands geographically the cross-cultural quotient keeps increasing. Based on our experience of managing such companies, below were some of our lessons:

- **Bad management styles and practices are exacerbated in global contexts**
  Frankly, what is often attributed to cultural incompatibility or cultural differences can be laid fair and square at the doors of poor overall leadership skills. For example, managers who are perceived as

poor thinkers and communicators, or seen as being rude and unaccommodating in their styles in local contexts, will be perceived even more so in a global context. Active listening and walking the talk are important for credibility in any context, but in a global context, poor demonstration of either of these can be fatal. In other words, bad management styles get amplified in a global context. If you are leading a global team, pay special attention to Management 101 lessons.

- **Focus on results and not style when you evaluate or judge people**
  Don't pay too much attention to style and approach. This way you can prevent your judgement from being coloured by what in your culture is considered a superior style. If you think a little carefully, you will figure out that culture is really about behaviours/styles that people believe makes them successful. And beliefs about what behaviours/styles make people successful differ by region and country. For instance, in some cultures, free and even heated debate is essential. In a different culture, people express disagreements more diplomatically. Therefore, do not generalize or stereotype. Do not make comments on styles (especially on what is a right or wrong style), and do not impose your style and biases. If you judge people by what in your culture are indicators of success, you are asking for trouble. Therefore, stay focused on results and outcomes.

- **Caring is important**
  A common mistake that global heads make is book time slots for calls that are convenient to them.

This can make you come across as being callous and uncaring. Schedule conference calls keeping everyone's convenience in mind (or inconvenience by rotation, if you have to). Take time to build rapport. In a global context, debits to your bank account (using a metaphor from Stephen Covey's *The 7 Habits of Highly Effective People*) are swift. You need to build substantial credits patiently before attempting to do things that would create these metaphorical debits.

- **Don't let people around you badmouth teams in a different geography**
  If you let this happen, it will create walls and divides that will get worse with time. Nip such conversations and loose comments in the bud even if they are being made by some of the best performers (or favourite team members) in your location. If you don't, very soon it will degenerate into 'me and my team (in my region/ country) versus them (from a different geography)'. Once this happens, your authority as a global leader will start eroding. Take an example: a global function head is located in a country that has a culture where people spend long hours in office (not necessarily working hard or efficiently) and a part of the team is located in a country where people start the day very early, work efficiently during the course of the day and leave on time in the evening. The global function lead, with some instigation from her local team, could conclude (wrongly) that the other team is not hard-working or committed. When such conclusions find expression (often unconsciously), they can cause irreparable damage.

- **Consult extensively with local leaders and influencers and earn their respect**

  For instance, if you are the global head for a line of business and are confronted with a sensitive issue in a country, seek advice from the concerned country head. The country head's buy-in can go a long way in making you effective in leading teams from her country. If you are playing a global role, make consultation your second nature. As you build rapport and enhance credibility, the extent and nature of consultation can be toned down.

  This is not to imply that cultural differences don't exist or don't matter. They are important but are often used as red herrings to skirt and avoid dealing with more basic management issues. Most people who manage global teams in today's start-ups do so at a fairly early stage in their career, when they have not had enough time to develop sufficient understanding of culture. If they focus on enhancing their basic management skills, however, their ability to effectively manage global teams would be significantly enhanced.

In Conclusion

Andy Grove of Intel once said, 'Whatever success we have had in maintaining our culture has been instrumental in Intel's success in surviving strategic inflection points.' Many other business leaders have said as much. Despite this, it is somewhat strange that in the corporate world the understanding that most individuals have of organizational culture remains as amateurish twenty years down their career as it was when they started out. Interestingly, in this period, their understanding of strategy, technology, marketing, financial planning, etc., undergo refinement and sharpening!

As a result, the term 'culture', specifically organizational culture, is used widely and casually with little understanding of the tangible impact it could have on business. Start-ups, especially in the US, have been drinking the Silicon Valley Kool-Aid for far too long. Free beer, wine on tap, bringing your dog to work, bean bags and fountains in the office, yoga gurus, massage chairs and coffee lounges are all good to have but they do not define culture even a wee bit. In India, office parties, team outings, outdoor games have sometimes been taken to reflect culture.

Therefore, don't get taken in by a company's espoused values or visible artefacts like office layouts. They have no relationship with the culture of the company. Just because a company claims to be 'customer-centric' and has this value pasted in bold in all the meeting rooms just does not mean that it is customer-centric. Culture is almost invisible except to a trained eye! Go build that invisible stuff!

5

A Founder's Journey

Change will not happen if we wait for some other person
or some other time. We are the ones we are waiting for.
We are the change we seek.

—Barack Obama

Safi Bahcall, an American physicist and author, in his book titled *Loonshots*, offers several great insights, but two stand out. For us, these create those rare eureka moments when a long-standing fog suddenly clears and a pattern that you are looking for becomes apparent.

The first insight is about a simple mechanism that helps foster innovation in organizations. Innovation is not just about that one cool idea or one great invention. It is about getting a diverse set of teams to take the idea to commercialization and usage. The organizational mechanism he points out is about creating the right degree of separation between the 'artists' (dreamers and innovators) and the 'soldiers' (operators), and at the same time having strong exchange and feedback mechanisms between the two groups. The separation ensures that the two processes that march to totally different rhythms and call for radically different talents are nurtured and have enough focus. The continuous exchange and feedback ensure mutual respect, which is critical for testing innovation on the ground.

It is a simple concept but for its execution one needs to understand the nuts and bolts of how organizations work. Vannevar Bush was an American engineer, inventor and science administrator, who during World War II headed the US Office of Scientific Research and Development. In *Loonshots*, Bahcall explains how Bush, with the blessings of Franklin Delano Roosevelt (FDR), helped the US come out of technological stagnation. For centuries Europe had been the cradle for science and technology, but under the leadership of FDR and Bush the US quickly overtook Europe. To put it simply, he used the mechanism described above to drive collaboration between the military and research (both public and private). Bush recognized that breakthroughs that had the potential to change our world were born from the marriage between genius and serendipity and created mechanisms that engineered these forces to work for these organizations rather than against them. This resulted in hundreds of industry-creating discoveries originating in the US, including the GPS, personal computer, the Internet, pacemakers, MRI, chemotherapy and artificial hearts. Even the original Google search algorithm sprang from the system Bush inspired. In his book, Bahcall provides another example of how the moribund Bell Telephone Company was rejuvenated when J.P. Morgan acquired the company and appointed Theodore Vail as the CEO. Vail did at a corporate level what Bush had done at a national level.

Several founders and visionary leaders used this principle to create iconic companies. Bahcall says that the difference between Steve Jobs's first stint at Apple before 1985 and his second stint after 1996 was that he learnt to love both his 'artists' (Jony Ive) and 'soldiers' (Tim Cook) during his second stint. Being the quintessential 'artist', he had demonstrated utter disdain for the 'soldiers' at Apple in his first stint. However, during the intervening years he realized that mutual disrespect and disdain between two critical parts of the organization were what killed innovation.

One big component of the founder evolution is developing the art of bridging these two key groups of the start-up.

In most cases, the groups are not as radically different as technology R&D and the armed forces. They could be operations and sales, technology and business, delivery and account management, manufacturing and design, production and quality assurance, or medical staff and medical entrepreneurs. At a more complex level, examples could be industry and academia, or government and business. In each of these cases, it is important for the two teams to have mutual trust and respect. Things don't augur well for organizations where conflict is not contained or sometimes inadvertently fuelled. It is quite natural for a founder or CEO to have a soft corner for one of the teams based on his/her own background. However, if the leader is seen taking sides, the delicate balance needed for driving innovation, product quality, customer experience or plain execution, as the case may be, is lost.

We believe that it needs far more effort and focus to keep this mechanism going as the start-up scales. It is much easier to do it at the early stages. For instance, a start-up needs to introduce stabilizing mechanisms, such as audits, compliance, governance, reporting, resource-sharing, processes, etc., as it scales. These mechanisms can sometimes come in direct conflict with the forces of disruption that generate new ideas and products. It becomes crucial for founders to not take sides and create the right balance between these two forces.

Sometimes, the nature of problems and challenges that the organization faces as it achieves extreme scale tends to tilt the balance in favour of the stabilizing forces, which could eventually take control and choke the forces of disruption. This is one of the reasons why organizations grow bureaucratic and ossify as they achieve scale.

As Geoffrey West, a British theoretical physicist and a leading scientist working on a theoretical model of cities, points out in his book *Scale*, the nature of forces and laws that drive scale are such that they become inherently unstable after attaining a certain size.

The Ability to Think like a Field Commander

The story goes that the German military believes that all generals can be classified into four categories based on their intellect and diligence (hard work). Of these, the smart and lazy ones make the best field commanders in a war. They typically have a razor-sharp focus on the three or four things that really matter in any situation and supreme disdain for the ten other things that do not matter or matter little. On the contrary, the smart and hard-working generals make great staff officers as they can devote equal energy to every problem, without an ability to prioritize. The worst, of course, are the stupid and hard-working generals and not those who are stupid and lazy as one would ordinarily imagine!

	Hard-working	Lazy
Smart	Staff Officers	Field Commanders
Stupid	The Danger Guys	Innocuous

Another big component of the founder evolution is graduating from being 'smart and hard-working' to 'smart and lazy'.

Just to be amply clear, 'lazy' is used as a metaphor here and should not be taken literally. It actually describes an ability to work hard on the issues that matter most and ignore or delegate the less important ones.

Those in the top left-hand corner of the table above (the smart and hard-working) make for great staff officers who can write good research papers on warfare techniques and develop policy documents. Those in the bottom right-hand corner (the stupid and lazy) cause no harm. You can ignore them. The most dangerous, of course, are those in the bottom left-hand corner (the stupid and hard-working).

They tend to work on all the wrong ideas very energetically
and can lead you in the wrong direction. You need to be
most wary of them. Those in the top right-hand corner (the
smart and lazy) make for great field commanders. They
are able to stay focused on the things that matter, have
supreme disdain for the things that don't, and have the
ability to quickly distinguish between the two.

We have discovered that intellect is not very strongly
correlated with the ability to think clearly as one would
imagine. Obviously this begs the question: What is
intellect and what is clear thinking? 'Intellect' is an ability
to grasp issues and recognize logical connections, while
'clear thinking' is an additional ability to filter issues and
connections that matter from those that don't. Intellect
allows one to understand complex things. Ironically,
intellect also has a tendency to complicate simple things.
On the contrary, clear thinking is an ability to obstinately
simplify complex things and prioritize. Bahcall recalls in
his book, *Loonshots*, that Richard Miller, an oncologist
in Menlo Park, California, told him in a totally different
context that when Francis Crick (James D. Watson and
Francis H.C. Crick—the pair that discovered the double
helix structure of chromosomes) was asked what it took to
win the Nobel prize, his response was, 'That's very simple . . .
I know what to ignore.' Clear thinking is also the ability to
see through common fallacies and biases. A common one
is the 'framing bias'. Here is an example. An e-commerce
company introduced a loyalty programme. In a review it was
reported that customers who had signed up for it bought,
on average, 40 per cent more stuff from their website than
those who had not signed up. This statement was used to
justify the effectiveness of the programme. However, when

the question was framed differently—'Do customers who signed up for the loyalty programme now buy more stuff from us than they did before they signed up?'—the answer was a resounding 'no'. It turned out that the ones who had signed up for the programme were mostly the high-value customers in the first place.

Multiple people we spoke to in the ecosystem consistently identified five Indian start-ups in the recent past—Swiggy, Urban Company, BookMyShow, InMobi and BigBasket—that have demonstrated a razor-sharp focus on their core business and relentlessly ignored the noise and distraction. Vishal Gupta of Bessemer Venture Partners believes that the secret sauce for some of these start-ups is scaling supply with consistency and quality. Demand, in his opinion, is a bit of a commodity and is equally easy to create for anyone. He further believes that you need to build using a 'full-stack model' because that's the only way to develop great long-term customer experience that will make customers come back to you. None of these five start-ups worried a great deal about who was doing what or how much capital they had raised. They appeared supremely confident in what they were doing. It was like Galileo quietly sticking to his view that the earth went around the sun, despite the church threatening to condemn him as a heretic. BigBasket stuck to its full-stack approach, or an asset-heavy model, in its online grocery business despite the popes of the investing world choosing not to back this model. In the minds of these investors, only an asset-light model could scale rapidly. These investors were unabashed backers of the 'go big or go home' school of thought that could potentially create monopolies or duopolies. That was the only lens with which they viewed everything. With a hammer in hand, you are always on the lookout for a nail. Even when you see something more interesting, you can't recognize it because of the blind spot you develop. Very soon these investors, like everyone else, realized that an asset-light model was totally inappropriate because it broke customer experience at every step. The founders of BigBasket had very thoughtfully answered the basic question of: 'Why does a customer shop with BigBasket?' This helped them stay steadfast in their belief that only a full-stack model would work. All these five start-ups had answered the 'why' of the business very thoughtfully. As a result, they did not try to hedge their bets by doing ten other things simultaneously or trying to be everything to everybody. All five of them drove operational excellence in their core business through relentless focus. In the world of books and films, all writers are broadly classified as either 'plotters' or 'pantsers'. The 'plotters' have a reasonably clear sense of the plot before they start writing and no character is bigger than the plot. On the contrary, the 'pantsers' start writing before developing the plot fully. The plot evolves as they write and so do the main characters. These five scale-ups were the equivalents of 'plotters' from the start-up world.

To learn how to prioritize, try to consciously answer three questions from time to time: What do I need to stop doing? What do I need to continue doing? What do I need to start doing? It is not easy to stop what you are doing, nor is it easy to start something new. Habits die hard, but it is much better to go through withdrawal symptoms and deal with them than continue with the addiction.

Becoming Self-aware

Samuel Johnson, a British poet, playwright, literary critic, and distinguished man of letters, once said, 'Almost all absurdity of conduct arises from the imitation of those who we cannot resemble.'

Self-awareness is not a common trait. Take a look at the 2x2 below. By seeking feedback with an open mind, you can move from left to right in the table below and by being more transparent and frank you can move from the bottom to the top. Through a combination of the two, you can get to the top right-hand side of the table. Get there soon. And, as a founder, help other key members of your team get there soon as well.

	You don't know yourself	You know yourself
Others know you	Asses	Wise
Others don't know you	Irrelevant	Smart Asses

Those in the top left-hand corner have poor self-awareness. Others find it difficult to work with such people. They may be too self-aggrandizing or too self-critical. Those in the bottom right-hand corner tend to put on masks, play games, are inconsistent and often difficult to work with. They begin by putting on masks for others but eventually end up putting on masks for themselves. As Francois de La Rochefoucauld wrote, 'Those who are so accustomed to disguise themselves to others in the end become disguised to themselves.' If you are in the top right-hand corner, you are fun to work with. Both you and the others know what you are good at and what you are not good at. You seek help on time.

Our understanding is that teams with a majority of members in the top right-hand box are likely to significantly outperform teams that have a majority of members in the other three boxes. There is too much friction, conflict and undercurrents in the latter teams.

There are several simple tools and instruments that you could use to enhance self-awareness. Most of these instruments are fairly simple and easy to administer, and the outcomes can be interpreted effortlessly.

Find Colleagues with Complementary Skills

In Hindu mythology, the 'trinity' comprises Brahma (the creator), Vishnu (the preserver) and Shiva (the destroyer). In some ways this is recognition of the fact that no one is complete. The holy trinity exists in Christianity as well, though we (we meaning the authors) don't fully know its origins.

The most obvious way the complementarity has played out in organizations is through a CEO–COO combination. When Sanjeev Aggarwal ran Daksh, he understood that his strength lay in thinking clearly on a host of strategic issues.

Though he had learnt execution well, he wouldn't have necessarily focused on it if he had a choice. In Pavan Vaish, one of the co-founders, he found the perfect COO who could run the 'business as usual' with great efficiency. And that is what Vaish loved doing. Aggarwal and Vaish made a great combination. The start-up world is full of similar combinations—Mark Zuckerberg and Sheryl Sandberg at Facebook, Deep Kalra and Rajesh Magow at MakeMyTrip, Mukesh Ambani and Manoj Modi at Reliance.

We believe that while it is important to play to your strengths, it is equally important to have an appreciation of what it takes to do what you are not good at. Only with this appreciation comes respect for what the other person in the pair brings to the table.

Start-ups Go through Phase Changes, and Founders Need to Adapt!

In the first chapter, we talked about Larry Greiner's model that he had described in an article titled 'Evolution and Revolution as Organizations Grow' that appeared in the July–August 1972 issue of the *Harvard Business Review*. In the article he talks of five stages of growth of a start-up. Each phase begins with the start-up successfully negotiating the obstacles that had begun to impede the journey towards the end of the previous phase. Each phase comes to an end when the problems associated with it begin to show up and become impediments. The seamlessness of the transition from one phase to another depends upon the ability and agility of the leadership team in adapting to the needs of the next phase.

We have clubbed the first two phases broadly under the category 'start-up phase', and the subsequent three phases under the category 'scale-up phase'. The start-up phase includes getting the idea off the ground, creating the minimum viable product (MVP) and getting the product–market fit established. At this stage, it is the idea, along with the ability of the founders to hustle and get it off the ground, that matters. It requires a basic knowledge of how to build the product, the ability to evangelize and the networks to bring in the people who could help create and market a prototype.

If the product–market fit is great and resonates well with the users, they begin to actively advocate the product through word of mouth and social media.

If the team handles the surge in demand that invariably follows any great product–market fit, well then the start-up begins to move into the scale-up phase.

The next three phases are different nuances of the scale journey. Those interested in what these phases specifically entail can read the original article by Greiner in the *Harvard Business Review*.

From a 'Big-small' Company to a 'Small-big' Company

We believe a start-up graduates from being a 'big-small' company to a 'small-big' company after the second stage.

At the beginning of the third stage, some degree of process orientation and stability is very essential even if it means creating a perception that the start-up has lost some of its zing. This perception needs to be changed with education. The option of continuing with the chaos of the early days is not there even if some employees who had experienced and fallen in love with the hustle desire it.

On a continuum of hustle and speed, start-ups are at one extreme and very large mature firms are at the opposite end. The trick as you scale is to avoid going to either extreme. This is what will help to innovate and remain relevant. Moving to a decentralized structure by hiring competent leaders to run the business is a powerful enabler for scaling at this stage.

A start-up in high growth quickly feels the pangs of becoming a 'small-big' company from being a 'big-small' company. Some of the common symptoms of this transition could be process failure, non-compliance and regression to the original state when you take your eyes off. The same problem showing up again and again, conflict between the old timers and the new hires, poor communication between teams, etc., are some of the other signs.

When a start-up grows to become a scale-up, the founders and the rest of the leadership team tend to get a little out of synch with what is happening on the ground. People tend to tell them what they like to hear. They 'distort' the truth, a little bit at a time, by sugar-coating stuff. One senior executive at a unicorn told us in confidence that when he joined this firm, he noticed that the Net Promoter Score (NPS) being reported was +40. NPS is a tool to evaluate how strongly your customers would recommend your product or service to their friends. This metric is widely accepted as a good predictor of organic growth, though there are sceptics who disagree. An NPS of +40 is considered good. However, when he delved a little deeper, he found that the NPS was being gathered by those in front-end sales and the scores were being collated in Excel sheets. The NPS question was posed verbally to a customer and wasn't framed correctly either. Everything sounded suspicious. He made changes in the way this data was gathered. An email would now go out from the customer experience team (not the sales team), and responses were collated with a tool. To everyone's shock, the NPS dropped from +40 to −45. When he reported this in the leadership meet, he was told that was not the way NPS was computed because only unhappy customers responded to emails that sought feedback. He was asked to make changes to the process of seeking feedback. But the NPS framework didn't say that happy customers don't respond to the feedback question. The framework said that even delighted customers respond, and respond enthusiastically. How you deal with bad news and how honestly you seek feedback and work on it matters a great deal.

At some point of time in the scaling journey, the founders need to learn to deal with issues they wouldn't have anticipated or prepared for early on. Most founders, especially those from a tech background, unused to the hustle of life on the streets, would be very uncomfortable and agitated if they were issued a court summons or had to deal with the police or any government official. When companies become really large and mature, they have access to both in-house as well as on-demand specialists who are well-equipped to handle these situations. But at the early stage of scaling, when the start-up is neither small nor really big, it struggles with these issues. It is important for the founders to start proactively building relationships with various government agencies. It is equally important to anticipate and prevent potential PR disasters waiting to happen. There will be disasters in spite of doing your best. Sometimes a vicious competitor could even set it up—a dead rat in a food packet, a pitiable picture on social media of your delivery person lugging an insanely large bag of goods, a woman customer molested by your delivery boy, violation of road safety rules by your vehicles, an employee filing a sexual harassment complaint with the authorities and posting the story on Facebook, leak of a damaging internal email or recording of an inappropriate conversation being posted on social media. The list of possible disasters is quite endless. There should be a clearly identified and sufficiently empowered disaster response and recovery team that should immediately take charge and do damage control. The team must be trained for handling such cases. If cases like these are not dealt with agility and tact, they could spin out of control and create lasting damage to reputation. The society at large and the communities the company serves are more forgiving if the company is seen to be generally socially conscious and caring. Therefore, at some stage, understanding how to make CSR (corporate social responsibility) initiatives work for you is essential. CSR initiatives slowly become integral to the business. If your start-up is disrupting an existing channel or a set of mom-and-pop stores, it is likely that you would come under attack. Often, the attacks are motivated and driven by partial understanding of the impact of the disruption your company is creating. Therefore, proactive education of all concerned stakeholders is a part of dealing with this.

Another important thing to remember is that you need to be extremely frugal before the product–market fit has been established and hire people who can multitask. Have people handling overlapping roles if needed. Do not splurge on anything. Do not hire heavyweights unless absolutely necessary. Hire people who can punch above their weight-class and have fire in the belly. Operate out of simple and functional facilities. However, after the product–market fit is established and you are in a growth mode, make the right investments in people and other resources. Get tools that enhance productivity. Operate out of facilities that can get teams some serious face time. Lease or build facilities ahead of the curve, so that teams do not get randomly dispersed across multiple suboptimal facilities. The intangible cost of having dispersed teams is very high. At this stage, trying to over-optimize on people, facilities and other assets could result in losing business and incurring a huge opportunity cost. The intangible costs of having functions led by leaders who were good at what they were doing in their previous jobs, but have been promoted to higher roles without adequate preparation, can be very high, and this may not be very evident.

Founders also need to learn to both build and manage a board. Different investors come with different perspectives and timeframes for an exit. Some board members tend to be 'financial engineers' who understand how to 'capture' value, while others are 'institution builders' who are good at 'creating value'. At some point of time, it would be helpful to bring in 'independent directors' who come with a deep understanding of the domain or specific areas of corporate governance, which become important in the scaling stage. The Companies Act in India has clear guidelines on when a company must mandatorily appoint independent directors on its board as well as the minimum number.

Let's take the example of B2C (business-to-consumer) e-commerce companies in India taking away business from traditional retail stores. When this began happening on a large scale sometime in 2019, owners of these stores organized themselves to protest against the onslaught and made representations to the government. Such conflict is bound to surface when an existing industry is disrupted. The founders and the start-up must be prepared for dealing with this. Similarly, when B2B e-commerce companies began taking away business from distributors, the reaction was the same. In their quest for rapid growth, several e-commerce start-ups undercut prices big time through discounts, causing angst and real damage to the existing players. Not all price undercutting was driven by better efficiencies. Often it was a result of cash burn. This is recipe for open war. So, these are things that a rapidly growing start-up that is disrupting an existing set of players needs to watch out and be prepared for.

One of the roles of founders is to be perceptive to this slow change. Watching your start-up progress and taking notice of some of the defining patterns is in a way like watching a child grow. It is a slow process, and unless you are mindful and watchful you might miss these signals. It is important to recognize these signals and shift gears accordingly. This may entail hiring a few senior professionals to run key functions or instituting a key governance process or buying the next set of technology tools or putting your first-time managers through a people management 101 programme or maybe hiring your vice president, product management.

Control versus Wealth Maximization

In the February 2008 issue of the *Harvard Business Review*, Noam Wasserman of Harvard Business School published a paper titled 'The Founder's Dilemma'. In this article, after analysing a lot of data, he concluded that founder-CEOs who chose to give up control maximized the value of their stake as opposed to those who chose to retain it.

However, times change, new data becomes available and you can have different conclusions.

One of the big changes that a high-growth start-up sees is that a set of seasoned and independent-minded leaders from different companies and backgrounds come on board in a short span of time. Since they are independent-minded and have been successful in their previous jobs, they have their own understanding of the right way of doing things. The question that founders need to ask themselves is how much of the existing culture of the start-up needs to be aggressively preserved and defended and how much of it needs to be changed by embracing some of the good elements that these lateral hires bring in. The initial conversations play an important role in shaping and creating the right mix. Holding on to everything that the start-up did so far without being open to the good things that the new leaders bring in can kill the very reason for hiring them. The founder needs to play the critical role of assimilating lateral hires by listening to them and making them feel as if they own the place as much as the early hires. Founders in some start-ups are easily able to assimilate and leverage the strengths of senior professionals in a very open and transparent style. They hire the right leaders, empower them and complement their strengths. This places their start-up on the right foot for the next phase of the scale journey.

There is a problem when one or more of the co-founders is unable to cope with the increasing demands of a rapidly scaling organization. The solution to this problem often depends on the stand that the founders who are able to cope are willing to take and the risks of sidelining founders who are unable to. The role of the investors and the board is important here. The first step should be to create self-awareness for a non-performing founder. A 360-degree feedback carried out by a neutral and respected third party for the entire leadership team can be very helpful. Some founders tend to shield the non-performing co-founders for old times' sake, whereas some other founders are a little more detached and hold the interest of the organization above everything else and take the tough calls.

The question that the founders of a start-up need to collectively answer, when one of them is no longer the best person for the role, is whether 'control' or 'wealth maximization' is the bigger goal for them personally.

Charisma versus Low Profile

Everything else being equal, it is easier for a charismatic leader to inspire and motivate people for the good of the firm. However, if the charismatic leader is a bit self-centred or motivated by grandeur, it is equally easy to drive the firm in the wrong direction without much opposition.

Obviously, charisma is a double-edged sword.

It is common human behaviour to exaggerate the accomplishments of charismatic heroes. Alexander Fleming, a Scottish physician and microbiologist, walked away with all the credit for the discovery of penicillin. It is not common knowledge that behind the scenes there were two low-profile doctors (Howard Walter Florey and Ernst Boris Chain) whose back-breaking work and contributions were equal if not more than that of Fleming. Fleming was the charismatic hero, and his picture in whites peering down a microscope made for a great story. Newton didn't discover gravity. He just beautifully synthesized almost everything that was known until then. But every child is familiar with the image of Newton under an apple tree! But he is also purported to have said, 'If I have seen further it is by standing on the shoulders of giants' in an apparent reference to Galileo and a demonstration of some humility. However, he was known as someone who was arrogant and ruthlessly stamped out anyone who dared to challenge him.

Good stories are always in search of charismatic heroes in every walk of life.

In corporate life, charismatic leaders have often done as much harm as good. And this happens because their excesses are ignored for far too long before they are discovered. The fall is quick from that point. The list is endless.

In 2001, Sherron Watkins, a vice president of Enron, an American energy company, blew the whistle and warned the CEO about accounting irregularities. That same year, the company declared bankruptcy. She later remarked about the charismatic CEO, Kenneth Lay, and what was going on at Enron, 'The ship has taken a hit in the bow and water is gushing in. The captain knows something is wrong, but he makes sure the band is still playing and the cocktail glasses are still full while his ship is going down.'

The stories that have been trickling in about the founder of WeWork, Adam Neumann, and the governance issues at the company are a throwback to the Enron days. Some are surprised but some are not. But maybe if the CEO was a little less charismatic, things may not have remained hidden for so long. The same is true for Travis Kalanick of Uber.

Susan Fowler's blog unleashed a chain of events that resulted in his ouster.

Someone had once remarked that the difference between a cult and a sense of purpose is that cults are mostly about the good of the leader, whereas a sense of purpose is about creating a greater good. Charismatic leaders sometimes tend to consciously create an aura of cult around them. And when this happens, they can cause more damage than leaders lacking charisma.

In the book *Good to Great*, Jim Collins describes a concept of leadership that he calls Level 5 Leadership. According to him, Level 5 leaders display a powerful mixture of personal humility and an indomitable will. They are incredibly ambitious, but their ambition is first and foremost for the cause, for the organization and its purpose, not themselves. They would use every opportunity to focus a discussion on the firm and the cause, and firmly deflect any attempt to bring themselves into the centre stage. Therefore, you don't get to read about Level 5 leaders. They are anonymous and steer away from any personal publicity.

A charismatic CEO can certainly mesmerize clients, users and other stakeholders in the short term, and that can drive revenue growth. It is therefore very convenient for the board to go with the flow and play along. In his book *Bad Blood*, the journalist John Carreyrou describes in great detail the secrets and lies at Theranos, one of Silicon Valley's better-known start-ups. He tells the story of a company whose product, which was based on a dubious technology, was positioned as the next wonder of medicine through a carefully orchestrated fraud that rode on the charisma of its founder, Elizabeth Holmes, and was endorsed by a highly regarded and influential board. When charismatic leaders become all-powerful, no checks and balances work. It is therefore important for company boards and investors to recognize this dilemma that charismatic leaders can pose to the health of their firm and institutionalize strong governance mechanisms early on to ensure that the charisma is not channelized in the wrong direction. Such mechanisms have not always prevented blow-ups on account of bad governance but the probability of preventing them is higher.

Line Role or a Problem-solver at Large

In a blogpost titled 'Why We Prefer Founding CEOs', Ben Horowitz makes the comment that: 'Professional CEOs are effective at maximizing, but not finding, product cycles. Conversely, founding CEOs are excellent at finding, but not maximizing, product cycles.' Therefore, another question that founders need to answer at this stage is whether they should take on line roles that are operationally intensive and involve optimizing product cycles or whether their talents are better utilized as roving problem-solvers, constantly looking for ways to disrupt status quo and discovering new product cycles.

We have seen that where a founder comes from a generalist background, her ability to lead specific functions gets challenged at some point of time in the scale journey, and the company may be better off if the function is handed over to a professional who has handled this on scale before. The way a start-up looks at something like this can be gauged from the 2x2 that we will present in the chapter titled 'Human Capital'. Start-ups in the top left-hand box typically have a tough time recognizing this and getting a professional to head the function whereas those in the bottom right-hand box tend to understand this a little better. One of the co-founders performing suboptimally at this stage causes both tangible and intangible damage. Taking the right decision is critical for the next leg of scaling.

What to Stop Doing and What to Start Doing

As Henry Havelock Ellis, an English physician, eugenicist, writer, progressive intellectual and social reformer, once said, 'All the art of living lies in a fine mingling of letting go and holding on.' In the early stages, founders are often so obsessed and preoccupied with fixing mission-critical issues that they just don't seem to spend any time on creating capability and capacity. As a result, they end up moving from one crisis to another. Actually, this could be quite invigorating and intoxicating. It takes some time to see through the futility of this approach. It may take some convincing to get them to change. Some of the founders obviously worry that if they give up this heady mix of unending everyday hustle they would have nothing else to do.

Start prioritizing and stay focused. Don't let noise distract you. Use meetings to reinforce key messages, drive values, spot talent, teach, coach and make decisions. Start doing things that build a long-term reputation for you company. Start hiring people who know their job better than you do and empower them. Spot gaps in organizational capabilities and start building them. Understand the power of creating the right organizational structures. Some structures work better at creating the right degree of ownership and separation than the others.

Stop trying to solve every problem because you love it. Stop taking on the monkeys of others. Stop being populist and be guided a little more by policy. Stop drinking with special friends within your organization.

Continue to drive agility, speed and a sense of urgency. Continue to stand up for the right things. Continue to be impatient for actions and results.

In a podcast with Siddhartha Ahluwalia of Prime Venture Partners, Gaurav Munjal, founder of Unacademy, describes his evolution eloquently. He says that in his prior venture he hired too many people too fast and was not mindful of the burn. He wasn't good at providing feedback, which was a public affair. Today he is thoughtful about hiring. He still provides feedback in senior leadership team meetings, but with the relatively junior members of the team, he makes it a one-on-one affair. He was aggressive earlier and had strong opinions about everything, and would get terribly upset if something was not done his way. But today he has evolved and learnt the value of patience, diversity of views and tolerance. He allows people to figure out the solutions on their own, because telling them what to do neither develops their skills nor is it a scalable approach. His favourite quote is, 'Mastery is not a destination, it's a process and it's a journey.' Munjal has found reading to be a good habit and a way of discovering lessons, both in failure and success, from other entrepreneurs.

Stick to Your Philosophy or Experiment with New Ways

This is possibly the toughest choice. It is important to remember the lessons of the past, but it is equally important to figure out the change in context and whether you need to revisit some of your lessons. A founder can easily make the mistake of taking extreme positions—go too much along with the trends and flow or hold on to positions based on past learnings.

Marshal Goldsmith, a business educator and coach, told us: 'What got you here won't get you there.' And the counter to this is if you forget what got you here, you will never get anywhere. How do you balance the two? How do you let your imagination soar and yet remain grounded?

Even after Steve Jobs's exit from Apple, the company continued to post strong growth by creating new products like the Macintosh Portable and laser printers, among others. However, with the launch of the popular PC and the relentless spread of IBM clones, Apple was shaken up and began flirting with the new trend. Two CEOs could not turn the tide. Eventually, Jobs returned through the acquisition of NeXT and replaced Gil Amelio as the CEO. Like many smart product designers, Jobs too had realized that customers may not always know what they want, and what they want is always limited by what they have seen and experienced so far. And therefore, designing a product by asking customers what they want isn't always the best approach. Jobs had always believed in the power of imagination and creating a product so good that customers would covet it the moment they saw it. A good product fulfils a customer need, but a great product creates a new and irresistible desire! This was his deep belief and he stuck to this even in his second term at Apple. This is a classic case of 'if you forget what got you here, you will never get anywhere'.

HDFC Bank, on the other hand, is a great example of an organization doing something very different from what the industry was doing at the time to race ahead of the pack in a classic case of 'what got you here won't get you there'. Tamal Bandyopadhyay, the author of *HDFC Bank 2.0*, says that when Aditya Puri, the former managing director of HDFC Bank, returned from an extensive visit to companies located in Silicon Valley, he asked his team why HDFC Bank should not be coming up with its own technology-based payment solutions. Why should a bank cede space in payments to the tech companies was his question. His belief was that HDFC must be top of people's minds when they thought of money! As a result of his persistent questions, HDFC Bank soon ingrained a digital culture and made a big foray into mobile banking. The astounding success of HDFC Bank is a well-known story.

Create a Strong Management Team

A good management team is essential. In a multi-founder situation, it is somewhat common for the founders to have a strong personal bonding based on prior experiences of doing things together, or a strong overlap in beliefs and outlook. This can be good and can help in overcoming the pangs of early-stage growth. However, as the start-up scales, this can be a little damaging if the relationship does not morph to embrace a more diverse bunch of leaders and create a wider team with a shared vision.

The importance of this is absolutely critical, especially if you are trying to build a business that would last. If the intention is to 'build to sell', which is nothing to be mocked at, then this aspect is not very important.

Vishal Gupta of Bessemer Venture Partners believes that there can be no bigger barrier for scaling than when founders are obsessed about 'control' or are wary of hiring people smarter than themselves.

Teams take time to fire on all cylinders. In 1965, Bruce Tuckman, an educational psychologist, identified five stages that teams go through, namely, Orientation (Forming Stage), Power Struggle (Storming Stage), Cooperation and Integration (Norming Stage), Synergy (Performing Stage), and finally Closure (Adjourning Stage).

Management teams, too, go through these different phases. It is important for founders to accelerate each phase of this journey through transparency, participation, empowerment, stepping back and letting go without allowing things to slip or regress.

Several individuals who are CXOs in their respective start-ups have reached out to us from time to time for advice on how to handle situations where they felt they were excluded from key decision-making processes. Their bitterness was evident. Some of them also felt that there were frequent and wild swings in strategies and focus areas. The language they used was a giveaway: 'Until last month we were told to focus on customer experience, but now the focus has shifted to optimizing costs.' There were phrases like 'we were told', which clearly showed a degree of frustration at not being involved in the thought process that led to this change in direction and focus. Every rapidly growing start-up is bound to go through these reversals and changes in direction from time to time. That part is not surprising. But unless you as a founder can make your senior-most leaders feel that they are part of the decision-making process, it's unlikely that everyone will push hard in the same direction with the same degree of commitment and belief.

Involving your leadership, assimilating diverse views and building consensus on the way forward is a skill. So learn to reach an agreement through discussions in your management team. Involve them and make them feel their opinions matter. Scale-ups that have the senior-most leaders putting all their energies into key initiatives are far more likely to succeed than scale-ups where decisions are made by founder/s and some board members.

Trust is the essential lubricant that helps this engine operate without stalling. Therefore, thoughtfully selecting those who will be a part of this team is as important as subsequent alignment and working together.

How Many Founders?

The general wisdom is that one is too few and four are too many. We tend to agree. Therefore, the sweet spot seems to be two or three. Several studies seem to endorse this conclusion. Obviously this does not mean that if you are a sole founder, you should blindly launch into a search for a co-founder or that you could multiply the probability of success by getting one. All it means is that successful start-ups with sole founders are rarer than those with multiple founders, and to an investor the probability of success is higher if there are two or three founders, everything else being the same. Obviously, the 'everything else being the same' is the spoke in the wheel that dilutes the validity of this conclusion. The challenges for a sole founder are many and need to be compensated by other factors. Similarly, more than three founders usually means some challenges in creating alignment and slowing down of decision-making. Successful start-ups that have four or more founders seem to address this unconsciously as the remaining founders happily operate on the periphery or eventually opt out.

Therefore, funding tends to be easier when the number of founders is between two and three, and their skills are complementary. Sole founders are viewed a bit suspiciously, but the suspicion can be overcome if after closer scrutiny the other data points seem positive. Similarly, start-ups with four or more founders are generally evaluated to see if there is a clear leader or a core leadership that is not in excess of two or at best three. If the number is three then the synergy in skills should be strong enough to overcome dilution in speed and direction.

Founder-CEO or a Professional CEO?

This has been an age-old debate, and one on which the opinions have seen wild swings. It appears that the majority of VCs today seem to have a clear preference for founder-CEOs, though some decades ago the same VCs may have argued for the induction of a professional CEO as soon as the product–market fit was reasonably well established. The underlying belief was obviously that the young founder/s had the ability to innovate and hustle to get the start-up off the ground to this stage, after which, in all likelihood, they would fall short of the skills needed to run a larger set-up.

In the same blogpost, Horowitz says:

Technology innovations are product cycles. Professional CEOs are effective at maximizing, but not finding, product cycles. Conversely, founding CEOs are excellent at finding, but not maximizing, product cycles. Our experience shows—and the data supports [it]—that teaching a founding CEO how to maximize the product cycle is easier than teaching the professional CEO how to find the new product cycle. The reason is that innovation is the most difficult core competency to build in any business. Most people view any truly innovative idea as stupid, because if it was a good idea, somebody would have already done it. So, the innovator is guaranteed to have more natural initial detractors than followers.

The counter to this is, of course, that the founder continues to play the role of 'chief innovation officer' focused on spotting new product cycles and areas ripe for disruption, and hires a professional CEO to efficiently run the 'business as usual'.

However, the number of start-ups that have been scaled to multibillion-dollar enterprises by their young founders is growing every day—Amazon, Oracle, Adobe, Dell, Salesforce, Siebel, Apple, Ola, Oyo, Swiggy, etc. The list of founders who have been able to successfully adapt is a long one. There have been a few start-ups that brought in professional talent with near-founder status to bolster management capability. Examples are Eric Schmidt at Google, Jeff Weiner at LinkedIn, Sheryl Sandberg at Facebook, etc. In each of these cases, the founder-level professional hires complemented the founders extremely well.

However, some founders were not able to scale and lead their start-ups after they crossed certain tipping points and had to be replaced. Some of these changes were amicable, others more acrimonious. Zivame, Housing.com, Flipkart and a few others saw board-led management changes at the top.

The bottom line is that each case is different and unique. Therefore, be aware of what has worked at other start-ups, but remember that you need to figure out what will work best for your start-up.

What you need to remember, though, as a founder-CEO is that if you decide to continue to run the show, you need to be very comfortable doing everything it takes to build an organization—town halls, communication, governance, compliance, long meetings and reviews, firing, coaching, business plans, etc. You can't just restrict yourself to your comfort zone.

Second-time Entrepreneurs

Everything else being the same, second-time entrepreneurs understand the challenges of scaling a lot better and are prepared to deal with them. Anand Jain, one of the co-founders at CleverTap, told us that he was able to leverage some of the lessons he had learnt at Burp in his next venture. He had learnt that setting out with the right team was a key success factor. He had learnt that generalists with high commitment made for good early-stage team members. He had learnt the importance of building trust within the leadership team, running the business frugally, not taking more money than was really needed or communicating and creating alignment with investors.

Since there is nothing like a failed entrepreneur, second-time entrepreneurs have been able to access funding more easily than first-time entrepreneurs across the world for these very reasons—the probability of tripping up on these issues is far lower, though the second start-up may still fail on account of other reasons.

In Conclusion

The journey of scale is really a scale-up journey of the founder/s. Founders need to unlearn and relearn a lot of stuff along the way. Every founder is different and scales in different ways. By all accounts, Steve Jobs remained close to being a jerk all his life. The biggest change he made in his style was to acknowledge the 'soldiers', and mastered the art of getting them to work with the 'artists'.

At Infosys, Nandan Nilekani evolved to learn the complex art of managing multiple and very diverse stakeholders and being an inspiration for each one of them. He could inspire the consulting teams and provide them with a vision and at the same time walk into a client meeting with a Fortune 50 company and blow away their leadership team with his thoughts on the future of technology. All this did not happen from Day 1. He learnt and evolved every day. Under his leadership, Infosys scaled new heights. He mastered the art of seeing the big picture and recognized patterns much before they became clear to the rest. He took this skill to create Aadhaar, one of the world's most envied citizens' identity programmes which became a game changer of sorts. Executing on scale in a corporate setting is one thing but executing on scale in a government project is a different kettle of fish. Like Bill Gates, he now takes these learnings to drive social transformation.

Explore your own aspirations, motivations and passions honestly. Learn and grow along the way. Discard some baggage, and pick up new paradigms. Neither would be painless. Finally, we'd like to close this chapter with a quote by the French poet and novelist Anatole France, 'All changes, even the most longed for, have their melancholy; for what we leave behind us is a part of ourselves; we must die to one life before we can enter another.'

Go out and find the joy in your life!

6

The Alternative to 'Go Big' Cannot Be 'Go Home'

I will tell you how to become rich. Close the doors. Be fearful when others are greedy. Be greedy when others are fearful.

—Warren Buffett

'Go big or go home' is a relatively recent approach to investing and business building that has its genesis in tech entrepreneurship of the 1990s. It has emerged as one of the new mantras for scaling. The old-fashioned formula for scaling was broadly about growing profitably by fuelling innovation and efficiency along with creating stability and direction through a combination of culture, structure and people, among other things. In the last three decades, however, a new paradigm has emerged. It is broadly about scaling rapidly and getting to a leadership position in terms of user base by liberal use of capital (or cash burn), leaving the question of how to make the business profitable to be answered at a later date. A handful of extraordinarily successful companies that used this approach to great effect like Facebook and Google inspired several other entrepreneurs and investors to try and replicate their success with a similar approach. In start-ups that have taken this approach, losses tend to exceed revenue for a fairly long period of time, something that would have scandalized a traditional entrepreneur. Even traditionally built businesses do not break-even on Day 1, but this new approach is not about making early fixed investments that could be amortized as the business scales. It is about running a business with negative unit economics for an extended period of time to create markets where none may exist.

Robert Metcalfe is an American engineer and entrepreneur who co-invented the Ethernet and co-founded 3Com. He gave birth to the ideas of 'Network Effect', 'First Mover Advantage, and 'Winner Takes All', among others, by formulating a law that described the effectiveness of Ethernet connections. Even Metcalfe in his wildest dreams would have never imagined that his idea of the Network Effect would drive waves of irrational exuberance in the investing world. In very simple terms, Metcalfe's law merely says that the effectiveness of a network is proportional to the square of the number of devices. With the spread of the Internet, this law was extended to measure the effectiveness of social networks. The logic behind Metcalfe's law is pretty simple. The total number of ways in which 'n' devices or users can communicate with one another is nC2 (the number of unique pairs that can be formed with 'n' users or devices) and for large values of 'n', this is proportional to 'n squared'. The message underlying Metcalfe's law was understood in an intuitive way in a different but related context. It was common knowledge that you could win big if your product was accepted by the market as a default 'standard'. The benefits that would accrue as a result of being the 'standard' were humongous. Some examples of standards are Android, NTSC, PAL and Ethernet.

There has been a lot of debate on whether Metcalfe's law is a true reflection of the power of a network.

Tren Griffin, a prolific author on business and entrepreneurship, in an article in the *Andreesen-Horowitz* newsletter titled 'Two Powerful Mental Models: Network Effect and Critical Mass', writes: 'As software continues to "eat the world", network effects become even more important as a factor in creating a moat since that's the primary way software companies build a barrier to entry against competitors. That's why venture capital firms investing in software-based start-ups include network effects in the business attributes they are looking for. Nothing scales as well as a software business, and nothing creates a moat for that business more effectively than network effects.'

Robert Briscoe, chief researcher at Network Research Centre BT, in an article titled 'Metcalfe's Law is Wrong' in the *IEEE Spectrum* newsletter dated 1 July 2006, explains why Metcalfe's law caught the fancy of Internet investors: 'By seeming to assure that the value of a network would increase quadratically while costs would grow linearly, Metcalfe's Law gave an air of credibility to the mad rush for growth and the neglect of profitability. It may seem a mundane observation today, but it was hot stuff during the Internet bubble.'

For many years, there was absolutely no evidence of the validity or practical relevance of Metcalfe's law. However, some of Metcalfe's followers subsequently used the data from social network sites like Facebook and Tencent and showed that Metcalfe's law held true.

The 'go big or go home' theme would soon become a cult call from time to time. The kind that became popular on T-shirts and car bumpers.

The Positive Side of the 'Go Big' Theme

There is a very positive and beautiful side to the theme 'go big' (not go home). Ambitious and socially conscious entrepreneurs have deployed this approach to address some of the world's most complex and widely prevalent problems.

The World Health Organization was able to eradicate smallpox with this ambitious approach. India used the Pulse Polio programme where on specific days millions of health-care volunteers fanned out across the length and breadth of the nation to inoculate every child in the country. Polio has been virtually eradicated. There are social entrepreneurs who are motivated by taking a primary school in a village and imparting better education to a hundred children, and doing it better every year. There are other social entrepreneurs who are always dreaming of how they can invent an approach that can do this for a million schools in India.

Therefore, you need those who are deeply passionate about both the 'go big' as well as the 'go small' approaches.

Society needs both kinds of individuals. The alternative to 'go big' cannot be 'go home'. It was the hubris of the dot-com bubble era that mocked those who were pursuing niches they were passionate about.

Internet Enabled the 'Go Big' Approach Bigtime

On 12 December 1901, Italian physicist and radio pioneer Marconi successfully sent the first radio transmission across the Atlantic Ocean from England to Newfoundland, disproving detractors who told him that the curvature of the earth would limit transmission to 200 miles or less. Although Marconi was Italian, he did not get sufficient encouragement and financial support for his ideas in his home country and left Italy to settle in England. Little did Marconi realize that his detractors were actually right in saying that the radio waves could never trace the curvature of the earth. This didn't matter much over short distances, but over longer distances contact would be impossible. However, a previously unknown fact would come to Marconi's rescue. This fortuitous fact has been the mainstay of radio communication ever since. Marconi's experiment was a huge success. The fortuitous fact is that the upper layer of the earth's atmosphere is ionized because of the continuous bombardment by cosmic particles from the sun. As a result, this layer, called the ionosphere, tends to act as a natural mirror for radio waves. The radio waves that bounced off the ionosphere were received at Newfoundland. Luck favours the brave! This was man's big leap in communication! The next big leap would happen more than half a century later.

Sometime in October 1969 ARPANET transmitted the first message between two computers, one located in a research lab at the University of California, Los Angeles, and the other at Stanford. The very short message, 'LOGIN', which was only partially transmitted, was sufficient to crash the network!

The technology continued to grow in the 1970s after scientists Robert Kahn and Vinton Cerf developed Transmission Control Protocol and Internet Protocol, or TCP/IP, a communications model that set standards for how data could be transmitted between multiple networks.

ARPANET adopted TCP/IP on 1 January 1983, and from there researchers began to assemble the 'network of networks' that became the modern Internet. The online world then took on a more recognizable form in 1990, when computer scientist Tim Berners-Lee invented the World Wide Web. While it's often confused with the Internet itself, the web is actually just the most common means of accessing data online in the form of websites and hyperlinks. The Internet, on the other hand, is a network of networks or an infrastructure that supports the World Wide Web.

In 1993, the release of the Mosaic web browser made access to the World Wide Web possible. Mosaic was founded by Marc Andreessen and James Clark. Mosaic morphed into Netscape Communications Corporation that created the 'Netscape Navigator'. The launch of these browsers was a big leap in tapping into the power of the Internet and laid the foundation for the creation of a whole new generation of Internet companies. Andreesen later went on to start the iconic venture capital fund Andreesen Horowitz.

These browsers accelerated the arrival of the information era. From an information perspective it immediately created a level playing field and everyone could now access a seemingly endless treasure of information.

Growth over Profits: The Dot-Com Mantra

Most dot-com companies operated on the premise that if you could unleash the network effect through advertising and early adoption, you could quickly acquire market share. Catchphrases like 'get big fast', 'go big or go home' and 'get large or get lost' became the norm. More than a decade later in what would appear a replay of the events leading up to the dot-com crash, Vijay Shekhar Sharma of Paytm resurrected the 'go big or go home' catchphrase immediately after demonetization when there was a huge surge in Paytm usage. In the days after the spurt in Unified Payments Interface (UPI) based payments and the success of platforms like Google Pay that rode on this network, the phrase was quietly buried. The phrase in its initial avatar in the valley, and in its new avatar in India, had sparked off memes that were both funny and crass.

Market share and user base was the holy grail. The belief was that once you got customers hooked on to your product, you could begin charging them and they would have nowhere else to go. In other words, you could create monopolies that would earn super profits. As per Wikipedia, in January 2000 there were sixteen dot-com commercials during Super Bowl XXXIV, each costing $2 million for a thirty-second spot. The 'growth over profits' mentality and the aura of 'new economy' invincibility led some companies to engage in lavish spending on elaborate business facilities and luxury vacations for employees. Upon the launch of a new product or website, a company would organize an expensive event called a 'dot-com party'.

The Internet bubble depended on high bandwidth, and it was only a matter of time before telecom providers jumped into the fray and invested in infrastructure to support the growing demand for bandwidth. Laying of fibre-optic cables and 3G expansion was happening at an unprecedented level.

While later events would prove that most of this infrastructure was highly underutilized and not justified by a rational business case, one can't help but conclude that bubbles are both inevitable as well as a necessary evil in the eternal dance of creation and destruction in the world of tech entrepreneurship. If you build a highway for traffic volumes that would materialize fifty years from now, you are hardly going to be able to multiply your money, especially if you are paid based on usage. The project may not even have a positive net present value (NPV) and would be a value destroyer. But if you could sell a story that the projected traffic volumes are just round the corner, then you are in the game. The trick is not to hold on to the project for long but instead exit by selling it to an unwary and impressionable investor before reality becomes evident to all. So the brunt is on those holding the can when the music stops. And when such a company finds an exit through the IPO route, those holding the can are 401K funds and mutual funds, besides retail investors. 401k is a qualified retirement plan in the US that allows eligible employees of a company to save and invest for their own retirement on a tax deferred basis. Only an employer is allowed to sponsor a 401k for their employees. '401k funds' is the biggest category of investors. It is difficult to imagine why a company that is not yet profitable should be allowed to go public. On 9 November 2000, Pets.com, a much-hyped company that had backing from Amazon.com, went out of business only nine months after completing its IPO. In all these cases, it is the ordinary investors who are bruised and decimated; the ones who have put away their hard-earned money for a rainy day or have invested their life savings as a hedge against inflation.

Every bubble that bursts leaves in its wake large-scale unemployment, financial ruin of the working class, a long period of loss of confidence and erosion of demand. At some point in the future, when the economy recovers, the infrastructure that was created on the back of the irrational exuberance prior to the crash could actually help in rapid recovery by accelerating the scaling journeys of the next generation of tech start-ups. Ironically, this in turn sows the seeds of the next bubble. The dance of creation and destruction and the saga of extensive collateral damage continue! There is little difference between naivety and excessive optimism, both of which are essential ingredients for feeding a bubble.

The Bubble Bursts

Between 1995 and 2000, the Nasdaq Composite stock market index rose 400 per cent. It reached a price-earnings ratio of 200, dwarfing the peak price-earnings ratio of 80 for Nikkei 225 (a stock market index for the Tokyo Stock Exchange) during the Japanese asset price bubble of 1991. In 1999, shares of Qualcomm rose in value by 2619 per cent, twelve other large-cap stocks each rose over 1000 per cent value, and seven additional large-cap stocks each rose over 900 per cent in value. Even though the Nasdaq Composite rose 85.6 per cent and the S&P 500 Index rose 19.5 per cent in 1999, more stocks fell than rose in value as investors sold stocks in slower growing companies to invest in Internet stocks. An unprecedented amount of personal investing occurred during the boom and stories of people quitting their jobs to engage in full-time day trading became common.

By the turn of the millennium, there was widespread fear that the Y2K problem would lead to computer systems misbehaving and resulting in chaos, mishaps and disaster. By then computers were at the heart of almost every machine. This fear drove companies to feverishly work on rewriting millions of lines of code, creating a huge demand for low-cost coders from India. This laid the foundation of India's ultimate prowess in software.

But the year 2000 will be known as the year when the Internet bubble burst rather than the year that launched India's software and services industry.

On 10 January 2000, America Online (AOL) and Time Warner announced a merger. Leading newspapers, including the *New York Times*, carried pictures of Steve Case of AOL and Gerald Levin of Time Warner. The body language in the picture said it all. AOL was the senior partner calling the shots. Some analysts were sceptical about the merger but they were a minority. After the crash, when the merger came apart at the seams, there were scores of case studies and reams of analyses on what went wrong.

In exactly two months, on 10 March 2000, the NASDAQ Composite stock market index peaked at 5048.

By mid-April, it dropped by 25 per cent. By June 2000, dot-com companies were forced to rethink their advertising campaigns. The crazy bidding for ad-spots in the Super Bowl was waning rapidly, and the 9/11 attacks further fuelled the dot-com bust.

Investor confidence was further eroded by several accounting scandals and the resulting bankruptcies, including the Enron scandal in October 2001, the Worldcom scandal in June 2002 and the Adelphia Communications Corporation scandal in July 2002. Ironically, or almost expectedly, Enron had been anointed by none other than *Fortune* magazine as the most innovative company for six years in a row. There were jokes that Enron's innovation prowess proved to be in accounting.

We believe there are two types of individuals and leaders: those who have external anchors and those who are anchored internally. The former care a lot for what society thinks of them. Their behaviours and actions are often guided by external standards and expectations. They could be normal people for the most part of their lives, but once in a while, when no one is looking or when they believe they could get away, they may display behaviours and actions that would not meet approval. Those who are anchored internally usually tend to be a little more at peace with themselves and do not crave for endorsement or approval as much as the former. There isn't much of a difference between their actions in private and their actions under public glare.

We believe that the 'go big or go home' motto has a tendency to compromise on ethics and integrity far more than the traditional motto of building and running a business sustainably. Just to be amply clear, the 'go big' motto is more grounded and is an approach that ambitious but internally anchored individuals pursue. It is the forced choice between 'go big' and 'go home' that makes the big difference.

By the end of the stock market downturn of 2002, stocks had lost $5 trillion in market capitalization since the peak. As per Wikipedia, at its trough on 9 October 2002, the NASDAQ-100 had dropped to 1114, down 78 per cent from its peak.

After venture capital was no longer available, the operational mentality of executives and investors completely changed. Many dot-com companies ran out of capital and went through liquidation. Supporting industries, such as advertising and shipping, scaled back their operations as demand for services fell. However, many companies were able to endure the crash; 48 per cent of the dot-com companies survived through 2004, albeit at lower valuations.

PandoDaily (a web publication that offers technology news, analysis and commentary, with a focus on Silicon Valley and start-up companies) published a well-researched article titled 'What Fred Wilson, the Godfather of New York Tech, Learned from the Dotcom Bubble' on 13 June 2013. Some excerpts from the article are insightful:

> Fred Wilson of Union Square Ventures lost a lot of money in the dotcom crash. Everyone did. But not everyone spent the next three years trying to earn it back. Ultimately, by scrambling and salvaging with his portfolio companies, he managed to make more money than he lost . . . Working through that became the most formative experience in his entire career, he said . . . The result of spending 2001 through 2003 saving 36 bubble-era investments? A dozen of them didn't survive. Another

dozen were stabilized and sold for a small amount of money. The last dozen, including comScore, went on to create almost as much value as the companies which had sold during the bubble.

Fast-forward a Decade

The dot-com collapse was followed by a phase of consolidation and a period of 'back to the basics'. But very quickly, there was a different kind of bubble altogether. Bubbles are not just confined to the tech industry. Other asset classes are equally susceptible to them.

During this period, one of us (Hari) worked for Virtusa, an IT-services-cum-product company headquartered in Boston. When the Virtusa stock began trading on NASDAQ in the first week of August 2007 under the ticker symbol VRTU, it was a matter of great pride for all of us in the management team. Taking a company public with a listing on NASDAQ was like a dream come true for most of us. J.P. Morgan Securities was the sole book-running manager for the offering, with Bear Stearns & Co. being the lead manager.

We had barely learnt how to run a public company to a quarterly rhythm, and under constant scrutiny, when we felt the early tremors of the credit crisis that eventually brought down the edifice of the world financial order like a pack of cards. In an ironical twist, Bear Stearns, our lead manager, was the first to fall and was forced to eventually merge with JPMorgan, our sole book runner, in a stock swap that valued it at a fraction of what it was valued just two days before the merger!

Events unfolded faster than we could imagine. The Virtusa stock, like the rest of the markets around the globe, went into a free fall and employee stock options were soon under water. Clients began cutting discretionary spends; some even cancelled, and revenue projections went for a toss.

The housing bubble was the downfall of many companies globally. It was like a virus that quickly spread across the globe. No one was safe. Every bank globally was evaluating its exposure to the toxic securities that greedy investment banks had churned out and sold to gullible institutional investors by securitizing sub-prime mortgages. No one was beyond reproach, including the rating agencies that were supposed to be neutral. The rating agencies had colluded with the investment banks to give AAA ratings to these toxic securities and fool unsuspecting investors. Under an arrangement where the rating agencies were paid by those issuing the securities, maintaining neutrality needed an abundance of guts and integrity.

The one thing common to all bubbles is greed, which is the root, and the eventual victims are often the ignorant and the underprivileged.

When the credit bubble began to sort itself out, the next tech bubble slowly started taking shape.

In the chapter titled 'Organization DNA', we spoke of how Adam Neumann of WeWork and Travis Kalanick of Uber very quickly went from being eulogized to being fired from their own companies. Both these companies were put on trial by the public markets. While WeWork had to put off their IPO in the eleventh hour, Uber currently trades at a discount of nearly 25 per cent of its IPO offer price.

In the rise and fall of these two companies is a lesson for start-ups and investors.

To start with, it was obvious to anyone who cared that WeWork wasn't even a tech company. It was a real-estate company that used tech, just like BigBasket was a retail company that used tech, or for that matter Citibank, a bank that used tech! But WeWork got away with all the hype around 'network effect' and 'winner takes all' that went into tech company valuations. No fault of WeWork. Adam Neumann had sold a story. Whether SoftBank genuinely believed this story or hoped that this could be packaged and resold to public markets is in the realms of speculation.

There were some doubts about the eventual profitability of Uber's model. There was no doubt that Uber was solving a serious urban problem, but the question was about the valuations this business model could support.

So, some of the excesses of the last tech bubble were again being played out but not on a similar scale.

If VC firms see an IPO as the real exit when they invest, things cannot go horribly wrong because public markets tend to be rational, at least most of the time. Therefore, the assumptions the VC firm makes about the future of the business it invests in also tends to be more realistic. However, when it sees a buyout by a mega fund like SoftBank as the default exit option, complacency sets in and things can go wrong. In some ways, SoftBank was single-handedly feeding this new bubble.

In our opinion, it is the time of reckoning for e-commerce and related start-ups in India. Many of them have seen valuations skyrocket to levels that just cannot be justified by fundamentals or common sense. Some of them are soon likely to face the woes that WeWork has. There is no doubt that many e-commerce start-ups are solving some genuine problems. However, growing a company to solve a real problem in a sustainable way takes time.

The trouble is that some of the ideas on which e-commerce start-ups in India are founded create the hallucination of a 'network effect' with a winner-takes-all outcome. The underlying belief is if you get ahead of the competition in terms of customer acquisition, irrespective of how you acquire them, the customers would stick with you even after you remove the discounts because they have nowhere else to go. This is a questionable assumption.

We (Shradha Sharma and T.N. Hari) explain in our book, *Cut the Crap and Jargon: Lessons from the Start-up Trenches*, that large funds such as SoftBank's Vision Fund are unlikely to return much more than the original corpus to their limited partners (LPs) for the simple reason that such funds are simply unviable when managed under one decision-making umbrella. Shradha Sharma is the founder and CEO of YourStory, an online publication that has contributed significantly to the growth of the start-up ecosystem in India. It is simply too big to succeed. You cannot will a market into existence. A dog-walking start-up with $300 million funding cannot create a ten times larger market for dog-walking.

In an article in *Livemint* dated 31 October 2019, Salman S.H. reported that Dunzo's net loss in FY2019 ballooned to nearly Rs 167 crore against an operational revenue of under Rs 77 lakh. This is the story with many other e-commerce start-ups in India that are burning cash far in excess of their revenue. Markets created on the back of sheer discounts can never be sustained. Only those with a cash burn that is a fraction of the revenue with a clear path to profitability have a chance of emerging successful.

Some of us may have heard of OLX, a start-up that was built around creating a marketplace for used furniture. It was a great idea, but in the greed to scale rapidly and create an illusion of growth, they began offering free logistics. Customers were smart and executed sham transactions and availed of free movement of household goods.

The counter to all this is that it is a free market and public money is not involved, so why bother? A free market is all about making bets. Anyone who believes the market is overvalued is allowed to sell short and make money if the belief is true. As long as there are large funds that are overvaluing some private companies, there will be entrepreneurs who will sell short their own stock and make money.

It takes time, effort and deep commitment to deliver the kind of consistent customer experience that creates a lasting enterprise. James C. Collins and Jerry I. Porras have devoted a book towards describing this: *Built to Last*. We would stick our necks out and say that many e-commerce unicorns will see their valuations shrink to a fraction of their peak before 2022.

User acquisition has again become a hot pursuit and somewhat of an end in itself. It is believed that once you have a large enough user base, you can find a way of monetizing it. This has always been a very powerful argument and an attractive proposition on paper. Assume you own a company that creates content for, say, HR professionals, and your content has become popular. You could then believe that your publication could be a powerful gateway to HR professionals and hence can charge companies who may want to influence or even sell products and services to this community of HR professionals. Start-ups too soon realized that monetizing a user base wasn't as easy as one would imagine. The other way of monetization was to eventually start charging users for the content. Start-ups also realized that paying users were a rare breed.

Wild Swings in Focus between Growth and Profitability

Scale-ups that go by the 'go big or go home' philosophy tend to go through wild swings. Many such companies in India, starting 2018, were either hiring big or laying off big. There seemed to be nothing in between. After the WeWork debacle, SoftBank suddenly woke up and issued a diktat to its portfolio companies to 'go for profits or go home'. Companies that had until now targeted growth at any cost were suddenly cutting costs and corners. They were laying off people in the hundreds and thousands.

The wild swing between growth and profitability is a destabilizer. 'Growth at any cost' creates fragility at multiple levels. It results in acquiring undesirable customers, creating poor experience for gold-class customers and excessive cash burn. It does not take long for investors to switch gears and start asking hard questions. One failed IPO is all it takes to reverse the sentiment. Scale-ups then start scrambling to get their unit economics right by cutting down on wasteful expenditure. This quickly results in large-scale lay-offs, along with withdrawal of discounts and cashbacks. It is kind of funny how the corporate communications machinery of these organizations justifies these lay-offs, usually stating 'poor performance' of the individuals as the reason.

Such wild swings are an inevitable outcome of the 'go big or go home' approach. A sound and sustainable business is built with equal focus at all points of time on three principles: growth, efficiency and foundation building. A little bit of special focus on one at the cost of the others is all right as long as it is done thoughtfully, but focusing only on one is pretty dangerous. 'Efficiency' is a catch-all term to include anything that results in improvement of margins and profits. Foundation-building, on the other hand, includes implementing a code of ethics, creating the right processes and governance frameworks, and technology platforms that will help scale seamlessly. Too little focus on any of these three principles could result in wild swings, which could be fatal.

Sidharth Rao, author of *How I Almost Blew It* and co-founder of Webchutney, a digital marketing communications company, told us: 'I've now begun to believe that today's media narrative of go big or go home, which loosely translates to get big or GTFO (get the f*** out), has a very condescending, intimidating impact that potentially discourages a very large number of promising entrepreneurs from building meaningful businesses that, in reality, have better odds of achieving personal financial stability for themselves . . . and finally, if you really examine your motivations and the kind of life you want to live, restraining your ambition may not be a terrible thing after all.'

'Go Big or Go Home' Has Infected AI and Big Data

We can see the early stages of a bubble in AI and big data. We have no doubt that AI is making huge strides and has been occupying some of the best minds of this century. On a lighter note, Jeffrey Hammerbacher, an early-stage employee at Facebook, may disagree. After a couple of years at Facebook, Hammerbacher grew restless. He figured that much of the groundbreaking work in computer science had been done. Something else gnawed at him. Hammerbacher looked around Silicon Valley, at companies like his own—Google and Twitter—and saw his peers wasting their talents. In April 2013, in an article on fastcompany.com titled, 'Why Data God Jeffrey Hammerbacher Left Facebook to Found Cloudera', Drake Baer quoted Hammerbacher: 'The best minds of my generation are thinking about how to make people click ads, and that sucks.'

There is a storm of hype around AI. Some of it, one can argue, is inevitable, but one needs to be a little watchful because it is entering everyday lives. Many of us are in positions, both in our professional as well as personal lives, where we need to evaluate the genuineness of claims to using AI, and if you can't separate the hype from the truth you would end up spending money on fake products and services or investing in start-ups that produce these products and services. They say that when it comes to capital markets, you are in the midst of a bubble if your driver begins to make stock recommendations to you. We can see that happening in AI now.

Let us first take a couple of examples of genuine AI products.

A few years ago, one of the co-founders of Liv.ai, a Bengaluru-based AI start-up, met us and demonstrated their product that used NLP to convert speech to text in multiple Indian languages. We had always known that text to speech was easy, but converting speech to text in multiple languages was a hard problem to solve. We were a bit sceptical, and more so because this was an Indian company. But when we saw the product, we were quite blown away. Soon, Flipkart acquired it and built their shopping assistant, 'Saathi', in text and voice interface to support shoppers in the smaller towns of India.

Facial recognition is another problem that has been solved and already has a wide range of applications that touch everyday lives, including unlocking one's smartphone. Work is in progress with image recognition applications in other fields, including horticulture.

Let us now look at a few examples of what we would call fake products riding on the AI wave.

A vendor once approached us claiming they had a test that could predict criminal tendency in an individual with an accuracy of 60 per cent, and maybe we should consider this tool to evaluate our delivery boys! Very tempting for a starry-eyed, gullible user sold on AI.

Let's dig a little deeper and subject this claim to a rigorous test. The test has a 40 per cent error rate which means that there is 40 per cent probability that it would classify someone with no criminal tendency as one with a criminal tendency. Let's now assume that the prevalence of criminal tendency in society is 2 per cent. So in a population of 100, you would have ninety-eight people without a criminal tendency. But the test would claim that forty-one people had criminal tendencies (40 per cent error rate on ninety-eight is thirty-nine; add the two real ones and you have forty-one). So, the error rate is actually thirty-nine on forty-one or 95 per cent. The accuracy of the test with this additional data point is just 5 per cent! Do you need anything else to decide whether you should pay this vendor and run all your new hires through a test like this!

On 3 April 2019, Eric Rosenbaum of CNBC (based on an interview with IBM's then CEO, Virginia 'Ginni' Rometty) in an article titled 'IBM artificial intelligence can predict with 95% accuracy which workers are about to quit their jobs' wrote that IBM was offering this tool to their clients. Rometty only said that its success came through analysing many data points. She did not explain 'the secret sauce' that allowed the AI to work so effectively in identifying workers about to jump. In our opinion, this is a false claim.

Those familiar with the 'butterfly effect' and 'chaos theory' would understand this well. Some systems are not very amenable to predictions for the simple reason that even the minutest variation in the initial conditions can result in a huge variation in the end results. In other words, a very small variation in the initial conditions does not result in a very small variation in the outcome! Weather forecasting is such a system, and hence one can't forecast accurately for more than a couple of days, irrespective of how much data you may gather and feed into a supercomputer. This phenomenon is more commonly referred to as the 'butterfly effect', where a metaphorical flutter of a butterfly's wings in the Amazon rainforests could cause a cyclone in the Bay of Bengal. Anyone who claims they can connect the flutter of the wings to the cyclone and actually predict it is talking rubbish.

Professor Arvind Narayanan of Princeton writes that 'much of what's being sold as "AI" today is snake oil—it does not and cannot work. Why is this happening? How can we recognize flawed AI claims and push back?'

He has classified AI into three broad buckets:

a) Areas where AI is genuine and making rapid progress like face recognition, medical diagnosis from scans, speech to text, reverse image search, etc.
b) Areas that are imperfect but improving like detection of spam, hate speech, copyright violation, etc.
c) Fundamentally dubious areas like predicting job success, recidivism, at-risk kids, etc.

The last category, which is really about predicting social outcomes, is essentially the snake oil being sold to gullible users and used as a pretext for collecting a large amount of data. Users are made to believe that magical insights can somehow be extracted from large amounts of data and more the data better the insights! Professor Narayanan claims that there has been no real improvement in the third category, despite how much data you throw at it; he further goes on to show that for predicting social outcomes, AI is worse off than manual scoring using just a few features.

We have no doubt that the inherent limitation in this area is imposed by the chaos theory. 'Data rich' is a phrase that has been misused of late to create false expectations. Those who predict social outcomes will no doubt claim that it is only a matter of time before it gets better. This is untrue. Some things can get better with time, but some ideas have inherent limitations. We would like to believe that the 'butterfly effect' is the equivalent of physicist

Werner Heisenberg's uncertainty principle at a non-atomic level. For those who were interested in physics at some point of time in their lives, Heisenberg's uncertainty principle is a fundamental principle that raises questions about determinism at an atomic level. It says that the more certain you are about a property of an atomic particle (say the 'position'), the less certain you become of a related parameter (like 'velocity'). This principle has found wider interest and has crept into discussions in philosophy as well. If small differences in initial conditions, such as those due to rounding errors in numerical computation, can yield widely diverging outcomes even for deterministic systems where an approximate present cannot determine an approximate future, imagine how much more indeterminate or irrelevant would the predictions be for inherently non-deterministic systems like social behaviours and outcomes! Vested interests will have a motive to create an illusion of being able to predict social outcomes using vast data. This needs to be dispelled!

Parallels in Entrepreneurship and Investing

There are a lot of similarities between investing, business-building or even career planning.

There are fundamentally two different approaches, neither of which is superior or inferior. It's a matter of choice and personal beliefs of the investor, entrepreneur or career builder. The first approach is largely about a long-term play based on certain fundamentals, values and beliefs. This approach also tends to be a little conservative in its assumptions about market size and the means to capture this market. There is very little 'timing' involved in this approach. It may or may not have a component of institution-building. The second approach is focused on growth and a race to a monopoly position, even if it means incurring high cash burn to create markets. While the first approach is cautionary and conservative, the second is about dreaming big and finding like-minded investors. A start-up following the first approach is unlikely to sponsor the nation's cricket team or buy ad spots during prime time during the most watched sports events. For a start-up that is wedded to the second approach, these would be preferred choices. Under this approach, rapid growth and valuation drivers override everything else. It is not that these don't matter in the former. It is the extent of focus on these that makes the difference.

In the chapter titled 'Organization DNA', we talked about two common cultures: a) one that comes across as strong and a bit polarizing in the sense that one is either a great fit or an utter misfit; and b) one that is soft and accommodates a range of personalities; where live and let live is the way of life. We have described the other indicators of each of these two cultures in that chapter. We believe that the first culture is what you are most likely to find in the latter organizations, which focus on growth, valuations and opportunistic forays, and emphasize on storytelling, whereas the second culture is what you are most likely to find in organizations that are playing the long-term value game. Quite obviously, this black-and-white portrayal has limitations, and there are examples of companies which have an aggressive culture but try and run their businesses in a sustainable manner.

In a later chapter, we will talk about how it is important to choose your investors because they too come with these two mindsets. It is not to say that an investor with one mindset would never demonstrate shades of the other. It's always where one is centred that matters.

In Conclusion

Most of us in India, especially those who are over forty years of age, grew up listening to melodious Bollywood music rendered by the likes of Kishore Kumar, Lata Mangeshkar and a few others. They dominated the scene so much that we didn't know that there were other equally good singers hidden in the mist beyond these few names. The power that these successful artistes wielded and the ease with which they could keep aspiring singers is well known. Similarly, there were a few authors that everyone read, a few brands that everyone knew and a few restaurants that everyone patronized. If you were an aspiring brand, or an aspiring artiste, life was an uphill struggle. The fixed cost of discovery and distribution was so overwhelming that no one would take a chance on you, not even yourself! Therefore, one couldn't hope to have a niche customer following. Hundreds and thousands of talented artistes died in anonymity and penury. This was the state of affairs in most other countries as well.

An equivalent of 'winner takes all' was the norm. However, the cause was not the network effect but the high cost of discovery and distribution.

Ironically, companies like Amazon and Google, themselves telling examples of a 'winner takes all' phenomenon, are giving aspiring craftsmen, passionate chefs, small brands, budding artists and emerging writers a chance to display and distribute their products at very low costs. You could create your own album and put it out on YouTube and expect viewers and followers! You could write an e-book, price it at whatever you wish and realistically hope to find a niche audience that absolutely loves what you write! You could whip up some delicious food in your kitchen and still be very hopeful of finding a niche and loyal customer base thanks to Swiggy. You do not need to set up a restaurant and worry about scale. It is interesting that the companies that were the product of a 'winner takes all' phenomena are now playing such an important role in democratizing talent and creating micro-entrepreneurs!

The 'go big or go home' theme will not disappear in a hurry. It is a deep reflection of unbridled ambition coupled with an alpha male syndrome. As long as this ambition is fuelled by private money, it may not be such a bad thing after all. The public at large, though, needs some protection when bad businesses built on this philosophy are sought to be palmed off to unsuspecting individuals.

Whether to swing for the fences or build a business the old-fashioned way is a choice one needs to make based on one's personal beliefs. Whether your style is that of a Warren Buffet, who usually believes in going 'long', or that of a George Soros, who made a billion dollars in a single day on a trade when he bet against the British pound, is for you to figure out based on your own personality and style.

7

Capitalization and Valuations

Lose sleep on creating value, not valuation.

—Deep Kalra, founder, MakeMyTrip

Sometime in the year 2000, Ajay Kaushal, Karthik Ganapathy and M.N. Srinivasu, who were working at Arthur Andersen, an accounting firm, came together to set up one of India's first payment gateways, BillDesk. This was way before online bill payments and wallets that enticed customers with cashbacks became a fad. In the year 2018, after a long journey of eighteen years, Visa took a minority stake in BillDesk and the company attained unicorn status. In these eighteen years, BillDesk had steadfastly focused on what it knew best and built a sound business. For the financial year 2017–18, BillDesk reported a profit of Rs 148 crore on revenue of Rs 929 crore. The average revenue growth in the preceding two years was 35 per cent.

The realistic growth and steady profitability were sure signs of a well-run business.

This was the way companies were traditionally built. Actually, when they were built this way, no one cared about unicorns (one billion dollars in valuation). Forget the fact that the term 'unicorn' didn't exist, the billion-dollar valuation was not a landmark worth announcing or celebrating.

At a recent start-up event at IIT Madras, Ajay Kaushal and I were part of a 'unicorn panel'. We were both rather amused at the level of interest in unicorns. We had assumed that the organizers of the event at which most of the participants were early- to mid-stage start-ups would be more interested in addressing the challenges that these start-ups faced. But no, a discussion on unicorns was what would draw crowds, we were told.

A unicorn is a mythical creature that does not exist! Despite this, the media and the ecosystem at large have displayed a disproportionate interest in start-ups with a billion-dollar-plus valuation! This excessive focus on unicorns has had both a positive as well as a negative impact on the start-up ecosystem. The positive impact is that they offer hope to every founder that if things go right and they execute well, there will be a huge jackpot at the end of the rainbow. The downside is that it is a false hope and a wrong incentive to build a business. In the past too, newer start-ups lost out on the much-needed visibility and PR (public relations) activities because the unicorns hogged all the limelight and media coverage. There weren't many business-building principles that these young start-ups could learn from either. In totality, we believe that the unicorn hype has done more harm than good for budding entrepreneurs.

As per a CB Insights research report, published on their website on 6 September 2018, titled 'Venture Capital Funnel Shows Odds of Becoming a Unicorn Are About 1%', 'less than half the start-ups that raised a seed round went on to raise a second round of funding. Every round sees fewer companies advance towards new infusions of capital and only 15 per cent of the companies in the cohort they researched went on to raise a fourth round of funding, which typically corresponds to a Series C round. Finally, less than 1 per cent of these companies went on to become unicorns.' This is a steep decline by any stretch. By this stage, most start-ups of any cohort would have ended up in the graveyard or would have been acquired. These findings were put together by following a cohort of over 1100 start-ups from the moment they raised their first seed investment to see what happened to them empirically.

Paytm took about five years to achieve unicorn status. In the next four years, its valuation increased sixteen-fold. This meant a doubling in valuation every year. And this was not a small start-up doubling in valuation every year but a unicorn continuing to double in valuation every year! Ola took about four years to be a unicorn, and in the next five years its valuation went up ten times. Starting 2008, several start-ups in India rapidly got the unicorn status.

There were many other start-ups that saw skyrocketing valuations in this period and were dubbed as the next unicorns or 'soonicorns'. Without exception, in each of these cases, the valuation was driven much more by heavy infusion of capital rather than through earnings. In almost every case, it looked like the investors were in the driver's seat. Some of the young founders came across as pawns in the hands of their investors, working hard to validate the investors' hypothesis about the market size, growth, network effect and consumer behaviour.

The Valuation of a Start-up Is Nebulous

The valuation of a start-up is an esoteric art fraught with assumptions, biases and a scarcity element. Reliable valuation techniques are applicable only after the business model stabilizes and the earnings pattern becomes more predictable. Valuations in mature businesses are typically driven by revenue (with a much greater weightage for recurring revenue), revenue growth and margins. In businesses which are still evolving—they could be early-stage businesses or multi-billion dollar unicorns— valuation tends to be subjective. Aswath Damodaran, who is arguably the most influential valuation expert in the world today, has written eloquently about the exaggerated valuations of some of the new-age start-ups. In a blog post (dated 9 June 2014) titled 'Musings on Markets—A Disruptive Cab Ride to Riches: The Uber Payoff', he says, 'If you are old enough to remember market fevers from past booms, you are probably inclined to dismiss the claims and the valuations as fantasy. I do believe, however, that there is a kernel of truth to the disruption argument though I think investors are being far too casual in accepting it at face value.'

Sometime between late September and early October 2019, Oyo raised $1.5 billion from its founder, Ritesh Agarwal, and SoftBank. In one of the most spectacular exits for early-stage investors, part of the capital raised was used to buy back the stakes of Sequoia India and Lightspeed Venture Partners. This transaction resulted in doubling the valuation of Oyo from $5 billion to $10 billion. In this lies the fallacy of valuations of VC-funded companies. If there is a private transaction in a public company between two parties involving a sale of shares at a price that is double the last traded price on the exchange, the market capitalization of the company does not automatically double! However, that is the case in a VC-funded company. And every large transaction at a VC-funded start-up comes with a set of complex liquidity preference clauses, which makes it even more unrealistic to value all the other shares at the same price.

In an article titled 'Squaring venture capital valuations with reality' in the *Journal of Financial Economics*, author Will Gornall and his colleagues developed a valuation model for VC-backed companies and applied it to 135 US unicorns. They discovered that reported unicorn post-money valuations average 50 per cent above fair value, with fifteen being more than 100 per cent. After adjusting for these valuation-inflating terms, almost one-half (sixty-five out of 135) of unicorns lose their status.

Connie Loizos, in an article in TechCrunch on 22 January 2020 titled 'Goldman Sachs's CEO just called WeWork's pulled IPO—which Goldman was underwriting—proof that the market works', says that in 2018 J.P. Morgan told Adam Neumann that it could find buyers to value WeWork at more than $60 billion while Goldman Sachs said $90 billion was a possibility. And Morgan Stanley was reportedly confident that it could be in excess of $100 billion. Everyone knows how the cookie ultimately crumbled. Even the experts got it completely wrong. Intense competition for underwriting a possibly lucrative IPO tempted these investment banks to stretch the optimism to an unrealistic level. Given the track record of some of these banks in the past, this behaviour was not too surprising.

When big investors chase big ideas and bet big on potential winners with a 'winner takes all' thesis, there is a tendency for private valuations to go wrong by a big margin. No doubt WeWork too would have eventually been profitable. The question is not whether a WeWork, Uber, Ola, Oyo or the rest would ever be profitable or not. The question is how long would it realistically take for the current valuation to be justified.

If the current valuation is far in excess of the real value, then at some point there has to be a correction. The correction can happen in three ways: a) a down-round when the company goes to the market to raise the next round; b) just before an IPO as in the case of WeWork; and c) in the worst case, post IPO when the share price drops significantly.

Three Likely Outcomes for Unicorns

We believe there are three likely pathways to the future for most of these unicorns:

- The first pathway is for unicorns whose current business model is reasonably mature, there are one or more strong moats, and the business is clearly headed towards profitability in the near future. Further, in this category of unicorns, there is no hype about the industry, market segment or a network effect. Because of lack of hype and realistic private valuations, the journey to being a public company through an IPO is likely to be seamless, with minimal divergence between the public and private valuations. A unicorn like BigBasket would typically fall into this category.

- Unicorns in the second category also have a mature business model, their moats are almost unbreachable, and their business is headed towards profitability in the near future. In addition, there is hype about the industry and a strong network effect in play. Because of the hype and the scarcity value, the private valuations are likely to be excessive. Therefore, there would be challenges in the IPO process—both pre and post the listing. In this case, the late-stage investors may have to take a hit. But some of them may have protected themselves with liquidation preference (LP) clauses. Ola falls under this category. Liquidation preference is typically a clause in any shareholder agreement that defines what happens when a liquidity event occurs. In the absence of this clause, the proceeds at a liquidity event are shared between the investors in direct proportion to their holdings. However, the liquidity preference clause spells out in advance how the proceedings would be shared between investors, and this is not proportional to their holdings.

- In this last category of unicorns, valuations are high, the current business model is still evolving, there are no clear defensible moats, and a late entrant could even be at an advantage. The reason the valuation is high despite no obvious moats is the belief that in this industry segment, the network effect is strong and scaling could be rapid. But the entry barriers are not strong enough, nor is the network effect adequately compelling to prevent large-scale migration of users to a new platform. As a result, this unicorn is constantly trying out new things and may come across as being everything to everybody. The outcome for such a unicorn is a big question mark. Paytm is an example in this category. To Paytm's credit, it has been extremely agile in making some right pivots. The demonetization of specific high-denomination currency notes was god's gift to the company. The very next day after the announcement, there were full-page advertisements in leading newspapers praising the prime minister for moving towards a cashless economy. The ads drew some flak and insinuations, but the mercurial founder's response on Twitter was quick and sharp without grandstanding. Paytm was on a high. Growth was exponential and all Paytm had to do was add servers. However, the UPI platform was always a looming threat. India had built the rails needed to move money at high speed and low cost. The rails were just waiting for fintech start-ups to ride on them. Suddenly, when a few private players like Google and PhonePe developed apps that used this infrastructure to move money directly between bank accounts, the power of UPI was unshackled. This posed an existential threat to Paytm, and its financials haven't been too inspiring either. It closed FY2019 with losses of nearly $570 million with revenue of approximately $470 million. While losses increased nearly threefold over the previous year, there was no increase in revenue. With such financials, a listing in India is out of the question. Listing on a foreign stock exchange is possible but the consequences are obvious. Listing in India traditionally has been more difficult than on some stock markets abroad largely because of the prerequisites around sustained profitability. It is valued at nearly thirty-five times the revenue multiple. And to make matters worse, this multiple is in a scenario where losses have been exceeding revenue! A zero merchant discount rate (MDR) policy, which the government of India has come up with, has left the entire digital payments industry in the lurch. Companies like Paytm and PhonePe need to revisit their business model. Only time will tell what the future holds for Paytm.

In the second and third category of unicorns, unless there is a steep and really quick rise in profitability and revenue, any attempt to go public could hit a cliff with sharp erosion of valuation. Given the kind of liquidity preference clauses that late-stage investors in these companies would have entered into, it could create severe angst for early-stage investors and even option holders.

Two Stories of the Triumph of Capital

The first story is about Ola and TaxiForSure. These two companies were founded just six months apart—Ola sometime in December 2010 and TaxiForSure in June 2011. Both were trying to do in India what Uber had done in the US: using technology to provide a cab on demand. Getting a cab was a big challenge in most cities across the world. This was true of India as well, including in cities like Mumbai and Kolkata that had a well-regulated hail-a-cab service.

The idea caught the imagination of users. Getting a cab was a big struggle for customers. They often ended up booking a cab for blocks of four or eight hours. Suddenly they could walk out of a meeting in an office or café in any city and get a cab with the help of their smartphones. This was an absolute delight.

This was a classic network effect business. If you could lock in a large supply, customers would prefer to use your platform because of easy availability of cabs. And if you could become the preferred platform for customers, the supply would automatically flock to your platform.

So the race to create these networks began in earnest. This needed cash burn both on the customer side in terms of discounted fares and on the supply side in terms of driver incentives. This was a strategy that would guzzle a lot of cash. Raising capital was key.

TaxiForSure was backed by Accel India, Bessemer Venture Partners, Helion Venture Partners and Accel US Partners. Ola had the backing of Sequoia Capital, Steadview Capital and Tiger Global. It was pretty much an even line-up. However, in October 2014, Ola successfully raised $210 million from SoftBank, which had emerged as the big daddy of the VC world and made big bets. Its bets often defined winners and losers, though, as subsequent events would show, they were not just vulnerable but often opportunistic and reckless. The SoftBank investment turned the tables in favour of Ola to a large extent. Until the entry of SoftBank, both Ola and TaxiForSure had tried balancing growth with profitability. Ola had focused a lot more on growth, while TaxiForSure had maintained a good balance between the two. While everyone knew that it was a game of capital, no one had anticipated that nothing else would matter. Raghu, one of the two founders of TaxiForSure, told us that investors in China and the US were still willing to fund the company, but at precisely this point of time there was one of those black swan events in which a woman passenger was raped by an Uber driver in Delhi. In a knee-jerk reaction, the regulators in India seriously considered banning taxi aggregators. Transport commissioners would walk into the offices of these companies, asking them to shut down or face the consequences. Funding dried up. The investors of the companies mediated a merger between the two to contain the cash burn. The only reason investors at Ola even considered a merger instead of allowing TaxiForSure to bleed to death was because of the looming threat of Uber acquiring TaxiForSure to boost their India operations.

Ola had the first mover advantage, and the number of customers who used their platform was higher than that of TaxiForSure. Because of the belief in the 'winner takes all' hypothesis in this highly network-dominated market, investors began preferring the one with a higher user base and number of rides. However, the endgame was some distance away and there was a good chance of TaxiForSure catching up. So, TaxiForSure too got some marquee investors. However, the outcome was settled when SoftBank brought a gun to a traditional knife fight and decided to back Ola with an unheard of amount of capital. In many ways this was the turning point and coupled with the black swan event it proved to be TaxiForSure's undoing.

The story of e-commerce horizontals in India—Amazon, Flipkart, Snapdeal, Paytm Mall and ShopClues—is somewhat similar. All these five players were playing a very high-stakes game. Each of them claimed to be different from the rest in terms of either the business model or the target customer segment. Only time would tell if the differentiation was real and sustainable.

At exactly the same time, in October 2014, when Ola Cabs closed a $210 million funding round with SoftBank, Snapdeal closed a round of thrice this amount with the conglomerate. SoftBank, which was until then a relatively unknown entity in India except in the VC/PE community, exploded on to the scene and made headlines in popular media with these two mega announcements.

The e-commerce horizontal play, like the taxi aggregation business, was about changing consumer behaviour and enticing them to buy online. While convenience, assortment and discoverability were all selling points of an online business, the Indian consumer didn't seem to care enough about any of these to migrate in a big way to online shopping. The touch and feel of the product as well as reliability was way better in a physical retail store. Discounts would eventually tilt the scales in favour of online shopping. Price was the touchstone for Indian consumers, and price discounting emerged as the holy grail for online marketplaces and aggregators. This meant immense cash burn and a need for unending capital.

While Snapdeal claimed to be a pure marketplace, ShopClues catered almost exclusively to customers in the smaller towns of India in terms of product assortment and pricing. The high point for ShopClues was when it raised $100 million from Tiger Global and GIC in late 2015 and soon entered the unicorn club. Tiger had been convinced about ShopClues being the marketplace of choice for millions of small local businesses seeking to reach consumers in the smaller towns and cities of India.

Nikesh Arora, then president of SoftBank, led the investment at Snapdeal in 2014 at a valuation of $1.8 billion. By 2016, its valuation had jumped to $6.5 billion. In January 2016, ShopClues, with a valuation of $1.1 billion, emerged as the fourth unicorn in India. Paytm Mall, with the backing of the parent Paytm, was also in the race. All the players were burning cash by the truckload. It was clear that this party couldn't go on forever. It was a matter of time, maybe just a few quarters, before there would be winners and losers.

This soon happened. Snapdeal began stumbling. Nikesh Arora had quit SoftBank. When SoftBank decided to rationalize its India portfolio, there was no place in it for Snapdeal. The latter could never build a leadership position in any category, and by 2016 it had slipped behind Amazon to the No. 3 position in the pecking order. Despite burning more than Rs 200 crore on rebranding and acquiring a slew of start-ups in 2016 that would supposedly unleash synergies, nothing really changed on the ground. By May 2017, it was in deep trouble and struggling to raise the next round of funding. It continued to slip behind its rivals, Flipkart and Amazon. Employee morale was at an all-time low. In a deft move, SoftBank, an investor at both Flipkart and Snapdeal, initiated discussions to bring the two bitter rivals together in a merger to take on Amazon. Part of SoftBank's plan was to hive off Freecharge, a payments start-up owned by Snapdeal, with another portfolio company, Paytm. In an article published on 30 May 2017 titled 'The seven sins of Snapdeal: how and where they lost their way', YourStory, India's leading start-up media journal, said: 'Unless you have been living under a rock for the past few months, you already know that Snapdeal is about to be acquired by its former rival and e-commerce market leader Flipkart. The only details that remain undisclosed are when and for how much the deal with Flipkart will be closed.' After many months of discussions and traversing several grey areas of governance regarding the rights of minority shareholders who did not have board seats, it was evident that this deal would not close easily. The final offer on the table was a valuation of $950 million, less than a sixth of the peak valuation. Flipkart was insistent on onerous indemnity clauses around representations and warranties, and some said this was the proverbial last straw that broke the deal. Snapdeal chose to stay independent and change trajectory to cut cash burn and turn around unit economics. Not everyone was happy. But everyone reconciled. SoftBank was thwarted in its plan and quickly went on to place a big bet on rival Flipkart by making a huge investment of nearly $2.5 billion. Snapdeal went down the path of focusing on the core business and good unit economics. It quickly disposed non-core assets. It sold Freecharge, which it had acquired at a whopping $400 million, to Axis Bank at a price of $58 million. Co-founder and CEO Kunal Bahl later wrote in a post on LinkedIn dated 8 October 2018: 'From near death to generating cash, from despondency to resurgence—it took a lot of courage, focus and discipline to turn the ship around sharply.' During the heyday of Snapdeal, Sachin Bansal of Flipkart and Kunal Bahl had frequent wars of words and even public spats on social media. The animosity between the two was well known. Time would tell whether the decision to stick it out by cutting cash burn was a commercially good one or one driven by personal egos.

Paytm Mall too struggled and went nowhere. It was no match for Amazon and Flipkart. At no point of time did anyone seriously believe that they stood even the slightest chance at giving a fight to either. ShopClues too saw a sharp decline in growth when it tried to control cash burn. It was also faced with leadership challenges that never got sorted out. It eventually merged with a Singapore-based e-commerce company at a reported valuation of $70–80 million.

Snapdeal survived by the skin of its teeth. Making a sharp change in strategy to a value play, it survived as a distant third in the race and disappeared from the limelight. Flipkart continued to raise money to support the cash burn, including a whopping $2.5 billion from SoftBank. Very soon, Flipkart itself was on the block and was wooed by both Walmart and Amazon. In the end it chose to go with Walmart. SoftBank turned out to be lucky and made a clean profit of $1.5 billion on its investment.

In both the taxi aggregation and the horizontal e-commerce industries, capital triumphed over everything else. There didn't seem to be much to choose between the different players. First mover advantage, having the right investors with deep pockets backing you early on, and sustained growth won the day.

In this see-saw situation, growth triumphed over unit economics. In both these cases, the drive for unit economics was put off for a distant day in the future. One could argue that Flipkart got lucky because Walmart was looking to launch into e-commerce to give a fight to Amazon. It would have been an interesting story if Walmart hadn't shown interest. In the ultimate analysis, though the founders of Flipkart had no role to play in the post-Walmart era,

Sachin and Binny Bansal came out as heroes. They proved many things to a sceptical nation and the world of venture investing and private equity.

Over-valuation Can Be a Burden

On 26 July 2016, Radhika Nair, a senior journalist, published a story on YourStory.com titled, 'How Jabong rode a rocket but landed in Flipkart and Myntra's arms'. The title said it all. Jabong was one of the coolest start-ups in the last twenty years. It started operations in January 2012 and within two months was airing TV commercials. In 2015, it was reportedly wooed by a large horizontal e-commerce company for an acquisition but talks apparently broke down because the offer price of $1.2 billion was not considered a fair one. In less than six months things deteriorated so badly that the best price that was on the table was $150 million. And in less than a year, it landed in Flipkart's basket—sold off for $70 million. The transaction was consummated in less than a week.

In the same article, Radhika Nair wrote:

> Yebhi, FashionandYou and a few smaller start-ups were the only other players in the fashion space when Jabong entered. Amazon had not made its entry into India, and Flipkart would launch fashion as a category only in late 2012. Jabong had entered with a swagger—spending foreign dollars on big-ticket ads and discounts. Myntra had launched its first ad campaign in 2011 but that was four years after it came into existence. No wonder the team behind Jabong was very confident about their potential to beat competition. A person who was part

of Jabong's senior management in 2012 told YourStory that 'we did not take Myntra seriously'.

Jabong was a case of excess capital driving reckless spending. This was compounded by serious issues of corporate governance. Governance issues continued to haunt Jabong until the very end, and Rocket Internet's forensic audit unearthed several such problems.

In a similar case, Webvan was an online grocery start-up in the US funded by the likes of Sequoia, Benchmark Capital, SoftBank and Goldman Sachs. Benchmark Capital, Sequoia Capital and Borders each invested $3.5 million in the company in a series A round in 1997. Sequoia, SoftBank and Goldman Sachs later invested $50 million, $160 million and $50 million respectively. Webvan raised a total of nearly $400 million in VC funding.

As per an article in CNN Money, '10 big dot-com flops', the company raised an additional $375 million in an IPO in November 1999, during the dot-com bubble that valued the company at more than $4.8 billion. Up to that time, the company had reported cumulative revenue of a mere $3,95,000 and cumulative net losses of more than $50 million.

After a mere three years of operation, it was running huge losses, estimated at more than $800 million, and filed for bankruptcy.

There are some very important lessons to be learnt from Webvan's failure:

- It was overcapitalized and overvalued at every stage. The investors piled on excessive pressure to grow rapidly. Every investor would make money only if the company could show rapid growth before the next round of fundraising. It was the same semi-Ponzi scheme at work. And Webvan had expanded rapidly to new markets without demonstrating operational viability or product–market fit in their first market. All the investors belonged to the 'go big or go home' school of thought.

- Webvan was founded by Louis Borders, who had no experience in retail. It then hired George Shaheen as a professional CEO. Shaheen was the CEO of Andersen Consulting, which had no operational background in retail. And finally, as the losses mounted, Shaheen was replaced by Robert Swan from GE who too had no experience in the grocery or supermarket business!
- Webvan splurged on infrastructure and signed up global engineering giant Bechtel to help create state-of-the-art order fulfilment centres with robots. Each of these centres were built at a huge cost. While they received a lot of PR, they were inherently too sophisticated to make sense in a low-margin grocery business.

After Webvan filed for bankruptcy, Mike Moritz, who represented Sequoia on the board, was eloquent about the reasons for its failure. It is a different matter that even after this, Sequoia never seemed to get its e-commerce bets in India right.

Too Much of Capital Can Be Bad

In an article published on TechCrunch on 20 December 2019 titled 'Do more startups die of indigestion or starvation?', Alex Wilhelm, a senior editor at TechCrunch, provides data and insights into how capital bloating can be harmful. While start-ups starved of capital eventually die, death due to bloating is not so obvious. There is an exquisite middle where start-ups hit the sweet spot and thrive. He quotes research that examined technology IPOs over a five-year period and found that 'the enriched or well capitalized companies do not meaningfully outperform their efficient (lightly capitalized) peers up to the IPO event and actually underperform after the IPO. Raising a huge sum of money is a requirement to join the unicorn herd, but a close look at the best outcomes in the technology industry suggests that a well-stocked war chest doesn't have correlation with success'.

Foie gras is a speciality food product made of the liver of a duck or goose fattened by force-feeding them corn with a tube, a process also known as gavage. The animals are typically slaughtered after 100-odd days. Foie gras is a popular and well-known delicacy in French cuisine. Some of the overcapitalized start-ups have looked like these ducks—fattened and being readied for a sale.

It has been a well-recognized phenomenon that pumping in too much capital too fast beyond what is essential to build a healthy and sustainable business can be damaging. It could result in inefficiency, large and idle teams, wasteful pursuits and experimentation, and non-accretive acquisitions. Traditionally, one of the biggest misuses of capital is in acquisitions. Both public and private companies have been equally guilty.

'Synergy' is the most widely used and misused rationale in mergers and acquisitions. Proinsias O'Mahony, a columnist at the *Irish Times*, in an article (dated 26 November 2019) titled 'If you do a big acquisition, the odds are loaded up against you', quotes Aswath Damodaran, professor of finance at the Stern School of Business at New York University: 'Synergy is seldom delivered in acquisitions because it is incorrectly valued, inadequately planned for and much more difficult to create in practice than it is to compute on paper.'

To this we would like to add that when you are sitting on a large pile of cash, irrespective of whether you are a private or a public company, you begin to hallucinate synergies that do not exist.

Paytm's foray into e-commerce is a clear case of too much cash driving reckless diversification. No one ever believed that Paytm had even a slender chance of making a success of its e-commerce gamble. Flipkart, Amazon, Snapdeal and ShopClues were already in the race and the market was being divided up between these four players. Being a late entrant made the task of wresting market share from these established players even more difficult. And worst of all, this meant taking its eyes off its core business of payments. While Paytm was busy building Paytm Mall, PhonePe and Google Pay were building alternate payment solutions that would pose a serious threat to the company's core business.

Snapdeal too ended up making too many acquisitions. Most of these acquisitions were made without much thought as to whether they filled in some gaps in its portfolio or brought in some additional capabilities that would give it an edge in the bigger battle. These acquisitions were made at peak valuations and sold off eventually in fire sales. It was the worst case of 'buy high and sell low'.

In Conclusion

Excess capital can help you kill competition and race ahead to the winning line. The adrenaline flow is high, the feeling is ecstatic, you are invincible and on top of the world. But it is a high-stakes game that needs resolve to avoid the wrong temptations. It also needs timing and good fortune. A few wrong moves, a black swan event, or the wrong timing can be fatal. At the same time, excess capital and inflated valuations can result in hubris, bad habits, inefficiencies and unrelenting pressure for growth. If you are on this playing field you need to play the game and not walk away, but keeping your head steady and playing with a sense of detachment can be helpful.

Getting valuations beyond what can be justified is like a pyrrhic victory. It puts you, the founder/s, straight on to the treadmill. You are running continuously to stay in the same place and return home (if you do) dead tired every day. You are on medication to calm your nerves and you have investors who are urging you to run even faster from the sidelines. Not surprisingly, the last investor is the one who is shouting the loudest and kicking you the hardest. In the ultimate analysis, 'return on capital' will always trump 'capital'.

Capital is a double-edged sword. Too much can kill you and too little can kill you too, although in a different way. The same is true of valuations. Raising money is inevitable, and so is negotiating a valuation. The temptation to get carried away is high. If you focus on building the business well, if you understand that sustainability of the business is crucial, if you keep your head down and stay focused on your value proposition and target customer segments, and, above all, stay honest and frugal, then valuations and capital make up for a little sideshow. As Swati Jena, author of *The Entrepreneur's Soulbook*, says, 'Frugality is not about austerity, it is about priority.'

8

The Human Capital

*No matter how brilliant your mind or strategy, if you
are playing a solo game, you'll always lose out to a team.*

—Reid Hoffman, founder, LinkedIn

Of all the enablers of scale, we believe the people side is
by far the most critical and nuanced. Poor understanding
of the human capital is the single biggest reason for
most promising start-ups, we know, getting derailed and
coming apart.

The table below captures our assessment of the typical
founder competence in a domain vis-à-vis the criticality of
the domain in the scaling journey. A deep understanding of
'customer' and 'product' perspectives are extremely critical
for scale, but most founders understand these domains
quite well. In fact, a start-up is almost always defined by the
'product' and 'target customer'. Hence, most founders are
well placed to navigate the challenges that crop up in these

areas from time to time. In contrast, most founders do not have sufficient understanding of human capital issues. The simple reason for this is that most learning in this domain tends to be experiential. Therefore, given the criticality of human capital and the relative ineptitude of most founders in this domain, it often ends up as the 'Achilles Heel'.

We have identified some of the most common human capital questions and challenges that start-ups face during the course of their journey of scale, and the choices in front of them.

Criticality in the Scaling Journey		Low	Medium	High
	High	Human Capital	Execution, Technology	Customer, Product
	Medium		Fundraising, Marketing, Analytics	

Typical Founder Competence

Here Are the Key Takeaways about Human Capital

- Lateral hiring is inevitable. What normally breaks is the assimilation of lateral hires and their seamless collaboration with the home-grown rock stars. It is important to get this piece right. Conflict between these two groups has been the nemesis of many a good start-up.

- Too few or too many lateral hires are bad. Getting the optimal mix and number is important.
- It is key to hire the right candidates for leadership roles. Timing is important, but more important is to spot the red flags in the hiring process.
- Most start-ups begin by being very homogeneous in terms of thought process. Founders and early-stage employees almost always have something strong in common that brings them together. This homogeneity is helpful in acting with speed in the early stages of growth, but need not necessarily be an asset at a later stage. It actually pays to build diversity into the teams as the start-up begins to scale.
- At rapidly scaling start-ups, some people start capping out in terms of capabilities and are not able to keep pace with the growing demands. So, when symptoms of things beginning to break begin to show up, it is critical to step back a bit and figure out whether the team needs to be strengthened or whether the leader needs to be replaced.
- Another important decision is whether generalists would work better or specialists would work better at different points of time for different functions.
- Learning and development is the cornerstone of creating leadership capacity, but start-ups are always brimming with intense activity and people cannot easily be pulled out of jobs to undergo leadership development. Separating learning from work rarely works, and hence it is important to integrate learning into work.
- Creating a culture of high performance, dealing with non-performers, coaching and designing the right feedback mechanisms are absolutely crucial for scaling.

There are standard frameworks that could be leveraged to strengthen these programmes.

Hiring Laterally versus Promoting Internally

One of the big questions that start-ups face as they begin to scale is whether they should promote internally or hire laterally. Employees who have learnt the ropes and proved their worth internally may have some limitations but both their strengths and limitations are well recognized. In contrast, the right laterals may be able to bring in all the necessary skills without the accompanying limitations, but there is always the risk of the unknown in lateral hiring. How should a start-up hire these leaders? What traits should they look for? How should they manage the inevitable tensions between the newcomers and the home-grown rock stars? How do heavy hitters who come from outside impact the culture of the company?

Hiring and assimilating lateral hires is a key success factor for a start-up to scale smoothly. Typically, a start-up begins to refresh talent after the product–market fit has been established and the founders see an opportunity to scale. By the time they reach this point in their journey, they have already recognized the inadequacies in the leadership team that could be an obstacle to further growth. It's possible that, while the early team is great at hustling and getting things done, its members often lack the ability to put in place systems to keep the ship stable as the organization scales.

This creates a sudden need to hire talent that has managed scale before. This is where the start-up needs to be a little extra careful because candidates that fit this profile are often very articulate and know how to deflect difficult questions. If you are a young founder, and if you haven't experienced or seen scale before, you might be easily impressed and get carried away by candidates who have handled scale in large organizations. You should know that everyone who has worked at a large firm does not know how to build for scale. Building for scale is far more challenging, and calls for a totally different set of skills, as opposed to managing in a scale environment.

The timing of the hire is crucial. If you get someone senior well before there is a real need and an opportunity for her to display her talents, people around her would begin to wonder why you recruited her. They might even get a little upset, especially when they get to know what you are paying her in cash and stock. At the same time, if you delay hiring this individual for far too long, you risk plodding along when there is a need for change in the trajectory.

Getting this right is critical and can make a big difference in the scaling journey. We'll give two real examples, of two different companies, one where we botched up completely and one where we got it right. In both the companies, we were looking to hire a global head of sales. The problem was the same. The founders were driving sales with the help of a young and relatively inexperienced sales team. There was a clear need for a sales leader who understood enterprise sales, the sales process, could manage and coach the sales reps, and who understood how to close large multi-year contracts.

In both the cases, after long and expensive retained searches, we seemed to find the right candidate.

An example of failure: Everything went well and everyone was impressed. He had done enterprise sales at two large services firms and had managed a large sales team in both the stints. One of the founders, a fishing enthusiast, even took this candidate on a fishing expedition to Cape Cod for a closer look in a more informal situation when his guard was likely to be down. The fishing expedition went well and the candidate progressed to the final set of meetings in Bengaluru, where the company was headquartered. When it came down to negotiating an offer I began to feel more than a little uncomfortable. He was pushing for business-class travel—when the prevailing company policy was 'coach' for everybody from the sales reps to the CEO—higher vacation days and a termination clause with a hefty severance pay. These were big red flags. All of us turned a blind eye to them. An offer was made and accepted. In less than seven months we had to let go of this individual. Everyone had noticed some of these red flags, but none of them were big enough to merit a discussion, leave alone a negative vote. I had, of course, noticed most of the big ones but chosen to turn a blind eye, hoping things would work out. They never do eventually! There are three lessons from this episode. First, start-ups at this stage are under tremendous pressure to hire quickly. Often, they delay something like this for long but once they have taken this call, everyone, including the board, wants quick closure. This results in some kind of a false consensus around an outwardly impressive personality. No one wants to be the fall guy to blackball the candidate. Second, it is extremely important for everyone, including a CXO, to be hands-on when the time comes for it. Being hands-on, with attention to detail, is not something to be ignored or taken lightly. Therefore, don't hesitate to explore this angle, however difficult and delicate it may be. Third, the way a candidate negotiates the terms of an offer provides great insights into the character of the individual.

An example of success: Vivek Chopra was once the CEO of Aditi Technologies. He was the head of sales of Wipro, North America, when we met him. He was everything the candidate in the last example was not. He possessed an interesting combination of qualities—confidence in what he knew, and curiosity and humility about what he didn't know. Informal reference checks came out strong. Despite his global savvy, the India-based teams found it easy to work with him. He helped redefine and restructure the sales function at Daksh that eventually took the company to a different orbit.

Too Many or Too Few Laterals

Taking a balanced view of the potential of an internal candidate for a new role is not easy. It is common to either overestimate or underestimate the potential depending on the lens with which you view lateral hiring. We believe there are two broad lenses with which start-ups view lateral hiring and believe that this is based on the emphasis the start-up and its founders place on ownership and accountability. We will use a 2x2 to explain this.

	Strong	Happy Family	Performing Team
Collaboration Mechanisms	Weak	In the ICU	Driven by Fear
		Weak	Strong

Focus on Ownership/Accountability

Companies that fall into the bottom right-hand box are those where people are held accountable—heads roll if things don't go well—but there is not much collaboration and synergizing between teams. The competition between teams and individuals could get unhealthy and each team is trying to overtly or subtly play the game of one-upmanship. They also typically suffer from poorly developed ideas, a 'hire and fire' syndrome, some amount of politics, high stress levels for employees and rapid swings (in everything). We believe that these companies tend to bet on lateral hiring a lot more. If a lateral hire fails to deliver, she would be let go of without much angst.

In contrast, companies in the top left-hand box show some kind of collective responsibility for outcomes. No one individual is deified when things go right or demonized when things turn sour. Non-performers get more than one chance and receive genuine support in upping their game. Typically, teams collaborate well but things still don't move fast enough because of a clear lack of ownership and accountability, resulting in everyone trying to do everything. This sometimes shows up as complacency, poor execution and poor performance orientation. But it is a nice and happy family. These companies tend to bet a lot more on internal candidates even if it slows down the journey. Since internal candidates often have their limitations, the founders tend to work closely with them and support them with problem-solving and decision-making. As a result, the founders may not have sufficient time to do what they are supposed to be doing. But the overall environment is one of a happy family.

While the first set of companies tends to be much more open to lateral hiring, the internal environment is not conducive to assimilating them and providing them the much-needed support and understanding of the historical context for them to deliver. It is a bit of a swim-or-sink approach. In such an organization, there is a continual trickle of exits of lateral hires, who are unable to cope. The second set of companies, in contrast, is almost always sceptical of lateral hires. In one of the start-ups we were associated with, the marketing function was weak and staffed by home-grown members who had started their careers as interns. Though there was a pressing need for a chief marketing officer (CMO), there was a tremendous reluctance to hire one. The founder, who was overseeing marketing, in what turned out to be a Freudian slip, commented, 'We don't want someone coming and teaching us marketing', which was actually the need of the hour. A Freudian slip is an unintentional error revealing subconscious feelings or beliefs.

Companies in the top right-hand box are best placed to handle the delicate balance of lateral hires and internal candidates. They also assimilate lateral hires very well and leverage their strengths. Both internal stars and lateral recruits learn through healthy interactions and develop mutual respect.

Assimilating Lateral Hires

Now that you've brought in some lateral hires, you need to immerse and assimilate them well into your context. A key element of assimilation is a series of early insightful conversations between the founders and the lateral hires that would quickly help each understand the strengths the other brings to the table and develop mutual respect. Both sides need to revisit some of their paradigms and definitions of what constitutes the right way of doing something. Great working relationships, where one unconsciously covers the other's back, take time to build. But unfortunately 'time' is a scarce commodity in a rapidly scaling start-up, and hence every opportunity needs to be used to create this alignment.

There will always be some inevitable tension between the lateral hires and the early-stage rock stars, who now need to report to them. These early-stage rock stars will have a tendency to test and undermine the new hires so that they can say 'we told you so' to the founders.

If you are a lateral hire, part of the responsibility for winning over these rebels rests with you. You need to earn their respect as they are the ones who have worked in the trenches and incubated the business if you want to be effective in delivering what you have been hired for. You need to also recognize and appreciate the tenacity, loyalty and single-minded focus that this extraordinary bunch of early hires demonstrated in getting the start-up to where it is. It is also important to quickly demonstrate that you can hustle as well as these early-stage stars, and that you additionally bring to the table a certain set of valuable skills that the old team doesn't have. As a lateral hire, don't start with being critical. If the norm is to watch TED Talk videos on Monday mornings, be a part of it. If beer parties, after review meetings, are a way of bonding, don't find reasons to skip them. The bottom line is, you need to genuinely start enjoying being a part of the team and what it stands for. Once you've established your unquestioned membership in the culture club, you can begin to drive the required change.

If lateral hires do these well, they quickly earn the respect of the rebellious rock stars. The founders also have a part of the responsibility for their assimilation and it is their job to facilitate a seamless transition. The founders need to recognize that one of the reasons they brought in these lateral hires in the first place was because they expected them to change the game and therefore help the early-stage rock stars understand this.

In one of the start-ups we know well, most of the lateral hires at a mid to senior management level failed quickly and moved on. This start-up fell into the top left-hand box of the table above, but took the call to hire these laterals because of a combination of board pressure as well some degree of realization that the current leaders had a few serious limitations. This start-up couldn't make a shift in mindset and move out of this box. Companies in this category are least welcoming of lateral hires, and that is what eventually happened. There was inadequate support during the assimilation period and there was also the problem of the founders blindly listening to the rebellious rock stars with whom they continued to maintain a deep connect. This ended up undermining the lateral hires who soon formed a clique of their own and it degenerated to an 'us versus them' situation.

Hiring and assimilating lateral hires as a start-up hits scale is the single most important success factor for subsequent growth. This is important even in the context of an acquisition where assimilating the founders of the acquired company is important to deliver the intended outcomes of the acquisition. An inability to do this well has been the undoing of many start-ups that failed to scale, and many acquisitions that failed to deliver.

Some More Red Flags in Leadership Hiring

The inability to ask smart questions and participate in a two-way conversation is a red flag. Some individuals just don't seem to have any smart questions. They come for meetings assuming that they just need to answer questions. When you prod and press them for questions, they may come up with a few checkbox kind of standard ones. And especially if you are the HR head, it could be, 'How would you describe the culture of your organization?' Irrespective of how you respond or what you say, they would just nod and not engage in a follow-up. *If a candidate for a leadership role does not engage in a game of brain tennis—whether* about the role, about the way the company or function is structured, about the strategic direction of the firm, about the competitive landscape, about what is expected of them in the first thirty days, or the culture, or for that matter anything insightful—*then it is a warning bell.*

Another red flag is if someone negotiates an offer incessantly. When we were looking for a senior enterprise sales executive at Daksh, we found a good candidate, based out of New York, and made an offer. In two days we received a red-lined version of the offer. It resembled an M&A agreement! We figured out quickly that he wasn't the candidate we were looking for.

Often, such individuals are lured by news about a start-up receiving funding or by the headlines it is making. They never bother to understand what this start-up, the one they are interviewing with, really does or how it makes money (or does not!). The best hires in our experience have, without fail, demonstrated energy and curiosity, right from the word go in a meeting. The interview is then never about asking questions and expecting 'correct' answers. It then becomes an insightful conversation that moves from point to point and topic to topic, steered delicately by both parties. Smart candidates are willing to challenge your assumptions and business model. They don't come across as 'wanting a job'.

Then there are the so called start-up lovers who just can't put their money where their mouth is. They say all the right things about the culture at start-ups and the thrill of creating something new. But the way they look at compensation is a clear giveaway. They subtly, or not so subtly, underplay the value of stock options. This is when you should try and get them to trade off stock options for cash compensation. The best fits are the ones who are not too finicky about the cash component. There are some who are ready to give up a few stock options in exchange for higher cash. These are the ones who are at least clear about their risk appetite and are honest. The worst are those who are not ready for a risk–return trade-off. These are individuals who are not willing to take any risk but want to be rewarded as well as someone who has taken risk. This attitude and philosophy reflect in the way the person approaches things once on the job. Such a person tends to be self-centred, covers his backside most of the time and is a poor team player. The correlation between the way a person looks at compensation and the subsequent behaviours on the job is very strong. No, we are not implying that negotiation on compensation is bad or that a candidate shouldn't negotiate. It is the manner in which a negotiation is conducted, the inability to make trade-offs and the need for instant gratification—in an ecosystem where postponement of gratification is the very essence—is what should raise the red flags.

We were looking for a COO for a start-up that was in a hyper-growth phase. One of the candidates we interviewed was a CXO at a large telecom company. We explained the fun and benefits of being part of this start-up that was redefining the space in a new industry. He was in complete agreement and said all the right things. To us it appeared that he had missed the boat in similar start-ups that had redefined industry contours in the recent past, and was now very keen to be a part of something like this. His current base was around $2,50,000. Hesitatingly, but surely, he stated his expectation from stock—$10 million over a four-year period! When we explored whether he was willing to take a pay cut, he said, 'My family is used to a lifestyle and it would be very difficult to take a pay cut.' In reality, he wasn't even ready for coming on board at the same pay with substantial stock. And it wasn't as if he was walking on water. He had a very low degree of self-awareness and an exaggerated assessment of his own abilities. He wouldn't have got on our shortlist even by a long shot, even if it weren't for the compensation mismatch.

Then there are the 'know-all' types. There is a serious problem if someone cannot easily say 'I don't know' or 'I don't understand this well' or 'this is not something I've ever thought about deeply' or 'I've never been able to ever do this well' or make some similar statements during the course of a conversation. If you end up hiring someone like this, it would be a struggle to convince her that what she is doing is not correct or that she goofed up. An important trait that helps make quick course corrections in the scaling journey is the ability of leaders to admit mistakes and move ahead. Nothing can be more frustrating than watching people waste time defending their actions in the face of overwhelming evidence that points to an error in judgement.

Informal reference checks can avoid a lot of trouble. If done well, they can help figure out some aspects of the candidate that you were not able to spot in the meetings or check out some of the red flags. What do we mean by an 'informal' reference check? The problem with most reference checks is that the referees provided by the candidate are very guarded. So, you are left with some oblique comment or a subtle remark that the referee refuses to elaborate on to draw your inferences. And this mostly leaves you in no better position than where you were. It is very important to get 'off the list' provided by the candidate. You can ask people 'on the list' if they could provide you with names of other individuals the candidate may have worked with. Not everyone would be open to do this but some would be.

An informal reference check is done with someone the candidate has worked with and who is also well acquainted with you or at least knows you better than the candidate. You could expect more candid feedback from such an individual. We have found informal reference checks extremely helpful.

Diversity or Homogeneity

Diversity is both good and bad. Homogeneity gives you speed at an early stage. In an article published on TechCrunch in 2013 titled 'Welcome to the Unicorn Club: Learning from Billion Dollar Start-ups', Aileen Lee, a venture capital investor and founder of Cowboy Ventures, says that one of the findings of a comprehensive study of thirty-nine unicorns was that there was very little diversity among founders in the unicorn club. This is the same article in which she introduced the term 'Unicorn', which went on to seize the imagination of the start-up world. Homogeneity in the team helps build consensus easily and move ahead with speed. However, the problem with homogeneity is that it creates cracks as the start-up begins to scale. There is a tendency to be blindsided by obvious gaps and flaws. Diversity can help bring these to light. Managing diversity calls for a willingness to be open and acknowledge points of view drawn from experiences and contexts you have not seen. And this is important because as you scale you see contexts you have not experienced before.

And by diversity we don't mean the standard gender diversity or anything of that kind. It is just diversity in thought processes and experiences. Diversity can be about getting a balance between those who are great at preserving the status quo and running a tight ship and those who are good at driving transformational change. You need those who can think with objective rationality and you need those who can sense subjectively. As a start-up scales, it is important to have these diverse styles and thought processes. Veering too much in one direction can create blind spots and rigid views that make it difficult to spot opportunities, make the right pivots when necessary or just take good decisions.

We believe that companies that are open to diversity in thought process invariably do a good job on the common diversity metrics of gender and disability as well. On the contrary, companies that are not open to diversity in thought process may hire women but end up making men of these women. So, diversity in such companies is superficial and only on paper.

For instance, in one of the scale-ups we were associated with, everyone in the leadership team was the analytical type. Even when the subject of discussion was brand positioning or price perception, in an instant the conversation would steer to specific product-level discounts. The team found it difficult to understand elementary human dynamics, define problems insightfully or see the bigger picture in some situations. Solving a problem has multiple steps: defining the problem, framing a set of plausible hypotheses, and gathering data that could validate or disprove the hypotheses. The pure analytical types are good at only the last step, which is the least important.

If you don't address the lack of diversity in thought process early on, it becomes difficult to change when the critical mass of leaders are clones of one another. Start-ups that are most amenable to diversity are the ones which have leaders who have a balance between the 'feminine' and the 'masculine' or the 'yin' and the 'yang'. The terms 'masculine' and 'feminine' have nothing to do with men and women, though when they were introduced they were abstract ideas based on gender. Assertiveness and goal orientation were some of the masculine traits whereas caring and collaboration were seen as feminine traits. Some women can have a very 'masculine' style just as some men can have a 'feminine' style. Start-ups led by very strong 'masculine' or very 'feminine' leaders are slow to embrace diversity. And when they do, the basic style often remains the same even when the gender mix becomes more balanced and the firm looks diverse on the surface.

The Choice to Hire Above or Below

This is a choice that a rapidly scaling start-up needs to make often. From time to time, some function or team is unable to keep pace and needs some rejigging. If the leader of the team is smart enough, she would figure out what needs to be done even before things start slipping. However, to our surprise, we found that in most situations the leader of the team or function doesn't easily figure it out. The symptoms are the same: commitments and promises are not kept, deadlines are slipping, everyone is overworked, internal stakeholders are unhappy, and the leader is lost in the weeds firefighting. To make matters worse, key employees in the team are leaving.

This leader needs serious help. In large and mature companies, roles rarely outgrow role-holders simply because roles tend to be relatively static, and the complexity of a role does not grow faster than the ability of a role-holder to learn to handle the additional complexity. In contrast, at high-growth start-ups, this is a very common phenomenon. We would call it the 'scale-up devil'.

If a founder tells us that she is seeing some of these symptoms at her start-up, we can confidently tell her that the team or function has a structural issue. The leader is working with a bunch of relative juniors who may be good at doing what they are told to, but not as good at independently handling complex problems or managing stakeholders well. The leader is lonely and does not have any sparring partner. There is no one to spend time with, figuring out if systemic improvements or key processes like 'requirements gathering and sign-off', 'managing a pipeline or funnel', 'resource allocation', etc., need to be put in place.

If the diagnosis is indeed correct, the choice is between adequately resourcing this team by bringing in people with the required capabilities under this leader or replacing the leader and then resourcing the team under the new leader.

This is a difficult choice. Most scale-ups struggle with making the right choice. Replacing someone who has been loyal and committed is not easy. To begin with, in most situations like these, the choice comes up after a great deal of trial and error, and nudging. The first reaction to such symptoms is to throw more people into the team (similar to the juniors who are already in the team). When this doesn't work, suggestions are made on process improvements. When this doesn't work either, the leader is advised to recruit a couple of more senior people. When this does not work because the seniors who are recruited also quit or the problems don't go away, there is a 'Eureka moment' when someone figures out that the problem is with the leader of the team.

In one of the scale-ups we were associated with, one of the businesses grew much faster than we had anticipated. The complexity of operations and management increased multifold. We noticed that the operating and customer metrics were gradually beginning to suffer and there was an increase in the number of customer escalations. One of the founders had to personally get involved in day-to-day operations. It was evident to us that the business head and his entire first line were unable to cope with the increasing demands of scale and complexity. The business head thought that the fault was with some of his first-line managers who he thought were unable to cope. Yet, he was doing nothing to either replace them or coach them intensely. For a long time, the top management too found it convenient to accept the argument that the problem was with the business head's first line. One or two changes were made, but the changes were half-hearted and limited by the ability of the business head to assess and select the right candidates. Things did not improve. Customer complaints kept increasing and there came a point when it was becoming clear that replacing the business head was important for cleaning up the mess.

In another example, in one of the large business units at Daksh, we had two very competent leaders—Ravinder

Singh Rana (who now heads Concentrix for Asia-Pacific) and Deepak Gupta (who is now the chief business officer at WNS). But the business was scaling very rapidly. While Ravinder and Deepak were outstanding leaders with a lot of inherent potential, they had not seen the kind of scale that we were experiencing and there were some early signs of cracks. So, we brought in Arjun Vaznaik, who was a much more seasoned hand, to head the business unit. One of the objectives and key results (OKRs) for Ravinder and Deepak was to make Arjun successful. The three of them went on to work very well together and the business unit grew rapidly under their combined leadership.

The diagnosis must be made quickly—whether to hire below and bolster the team or replace the leader. If you decide to replace the leader, you need to have the difficult conversation. The conversation is not about firing this individual but about finding a role that does not place so many demands, where she can learn and grow without breaking. Mostly it's not the individual's fault but the unnatural pace of growth. The leader can sometimes be accommodated in the same team after some tweaks to the structure. Once in a while, the leader demonstrates poor self-awareness and is adamant that the problem is not with her, and if you insist on the change, she might want to move on. In such situations, it is best to let her go.

In any case, it is important to ensure that this decision is 'process driven' and not seen as a whim of the founder. If it is, then the effectiveness of such decisions could be undermined. The process needs to ensure that the shortcomings show up in group meetings, which quickly help build a broader consensus on such decisions.

Generalists or Specialists

This is an important question. At an early stage you need everyone to behave like a generalist. Everyone needs to chip in on almost everything. It is more important to be able to hustle and get things done than to know a domain well.

But as you scale, you need to answer an important question: Who is really a generalist and who is a specialist? Some domains like technology, engineering, analytics, data sciences and accounting don't lend themselves to generalists. Anyone who wishes to work in these domains needs to first master their rigorous and well-established bodies of knowledge. Those who rise to leadership positions in these domains need to additionally develop and demonstrate some general management skills along the way.

In contrast, domains like marketing, sales, business, HR, product, program management, operations, financial planning and budgeting, supply chain, etc., are far more amenable to 'first-principles thinking'. First-principles thinking is essentially about questioning assumptions and asking smart questions about a problem before attempting a solution. Therefore, it is a powerful approach to solving problems not encountered before. There are established bodies of knowledge in some of these domains as well, but they are not anywhere as rigorous as those in the earlier domains. An MBA degree is a great example of generalist education. In fact, an MBA is mostly about reinforcing first-principles thinking and encouraging basic smarts. It is the approach that companies take with these functions that determines whether their bias is towards generalists or specialists. For functions outlined in the previous paragraph (like data sciences, etc.), every company settles on specialists.

Some companies tend to create a cadre of generalists that rotate between different functions before growing into senior management roles as fully rounded individuals. If you are still a start-up scaling rapidly and have not created a formal cadre, you could opt for this approach, where you rotate people across functions. Alternately, you could opt for minimal rotation and let people grow within their verticals.

We believe start-ups that rotate people tend to be better problem-solvers and can deal with cross-functional problems more effectively, whereas companies that opt for specialization even in these functions need founder intervention and energy behind cross-functional problems and interfaces. Start-ups that opt for generalists also tend to be more ambitious when it comes to growth, though, like for everything else, there could be exceptions.

In short, hiring people who are first-principles thinkers is generally a good strategy because the entire start-up and scale-up journey is uncharted and needs professionals with an ability to deal with situations that they haven't necessarily seen before. In such a scenario, the best bet is to have people who are smart with an ability to use first principles to solve problems.

Learning while Scaling

People in rapidly scaling start-ups are starved for bandwidth and time. Putting them through traditional development programmes that large and mature companies put their employees through simply doesn't work. Therefore, the fundamental design feature of a leadership model for a start-up should involve building leadership capability *on the job*. We are great fans of the 70:20:10 model for creating leadership capability, which essentially says that 70 per cent of learning and character-building comes from tough assignments and dealing with difficult situations; 20 per cent from insightful conversations and straight talk (mostly with your manager); and only 10 per cent through classroom training.

At Daksh, where we both worked, the monthly review meeting (MRM) was a forum for forging leaders. The MRM could be pretty intimidating if you were attending it for the first time. The questioning was hard, there was no mincing of words, no room for niceties, and the orientation towards facts and data was unrelenting. You had to hold your ground and defend your own point of view. Disagreement was respected (and the respect multiplied manifold if you could substantiate your point of view with data, facts or insight) and mute acceptance evoked disgust. If you survived twelve of these in a row, you could write a new CV. You learnt to develop a point of view and defend it. You learnt how to handle three questions that haunted everyone: 'so what?', 'why?', and 'what if?'. You learnt problem-solving. You learnt to handle aggressive environments. You developed internal customer orientation. No amount of classroom training in a leadership institute could substitute for this. In addition to shaping and forging leaders, this was a great forum for spotting leadership potential. Hence, succession planning and internal deployment on key projects became much more objective and unbiased. Quite frankly, you could judge a leader by the competence of her team, which was now visible to others. Some leaders were lone wolves. They turned up alone for most meetings. Some of them were even brilliant, knowing every detail, but one never knew who operated behind the scenes in their teams—who were the numbers guys, who created the beautiful decks, or who put together those wonderful insights.

In some scale-ups, leaders invite some of their first-line or second-line team members, who are not directly involved with the issue under discussion, to meetings and reviews. These individuals are invited to sit through these meetings to observe and learn how disagreements are resolved, how consensus is built, how choices are made, how problems are solved, how execution issues are handled, how plans are made and communicated, etc. All these skills can be learnt by seeing people demonstrate them in a live setting and relevant context.

Another tool for forging leaders is to set stretch goals and allow them the freedom to imagine how they would be met. Tough goals and stretch assignments are mechanisms to throw people into the deep end and see how they manage. Some of the leaders that we saw were very good at this—they pushed their people hard and right to the brink, but provided just enough support to prevent them from toppling over. Individuals who went through these successfully soon shaped up into seasoned leaders. The beauty of this is that if you do this, the individuals concerned would nominate themselves for the right kind of leadership programmes and show serious interest in learning some of the leadership techniques and frameworks that these programmes intend to impart!

Creating a Culture of High Performance

Advanced Leadership Consulting, a company that provides consulting on leadership development, in a post on their site, quotes Henry Cloud, a popular self-help author: 'If you are building a culture where honest expectations are communicated and peer accountability is the norm, then the group will address poor performance and attitudes.'

There are broadly three components of creating a high-performance culture, namely, getting alignment, setting goals and conducting insightful reviews, and having strong feedback mechanisms.

You create alignment by living and reinforcing values, and setting the pace and expectations in every interaction. Over a period of time, the team imbibes these into their DNA and way of working.

Goal-setting is a well-established tool for getting everyone in the organization aligned. It starts with sharing aspirations by the founders or founder-CEO. You can begin by sharing your aspirations with the executive team or better still co-create an aspiration. Aspirations are about the vision/goals for the next twelve to twenty-four months. This should be followed by a discussion on the constraints and interdependencies, and what each business and function needs to do for the company to achieve its goals.

Assemble a week later and have every function/business present its respective goals that dovetail with the company's overall goals.

There is a lot of jargon in goal-setting—OKRs (objectives and key results) and KRAs (key result areas) are just a few. But whatever alphabets and names you assign them, these are just tools or a framework to prioritize efforts and get individuals in the organization to pull towards a common goal. If one understands the principles and process behind this exercise of objective-setting (irrespective of what you call it), you are bound to execute it well.

The one thing we have learnt over the years is that the sophistication of a tool or a framework has little to do with its effectiveness on the ground. Those who understand the principles behind a tool manage well even without it. The tool merely makes the process a little more structured and efficient. And those who do not understand the principles behind a tool well enough are actually worse off with it! It's like providing a bike to someone who has no clue how to get to a place. She would probably end up at the wrong destination faster. If you haven't got your direction right, then you would probably be better off with poor execution rather than good execution.

One of us was recently chatting with a function head about his OKRs and was surprised to see a list of nineteen. And like a true engineer, he had assigned weightages to each. Obviously, there were some OKRs with weightages as low as 3 per cent. As we walked through the list, it was evident that everything he or his team was expected to do was on this list.

Any OKR list should not have more than four to six of the most important things that you need to focus on. The same goes for the OKRs of those who report to you. If people in your team are not attending training sessions they have signed up for, you cannot solve this problem by including 'attending training programmes' as one of their OKRs with a 5 per cent weightage! It may sound ludicrous but there is a tendency to include elementary things on the list of OKRs, which needs to be fixed by clear-headed and firm leadership.

Goal-setting needs to be based on certain principles. Goals should have some realistic stretch. Rapid scaling does not happen without stretch. There should also be a degree of predictability in the goals. This means that you understand what is driving your business, and that the goals you have set are not just a shot in the dark or based on a stupid sense of daredevilry. In fact, public markets sometimes punish companies that beat their targets by a big margin. They smell something fishy—either the company is sandbagging or they don't know what they are doing. There should also be a strong 'improvement orientation' in goals—improvement over a previous best, for instance. Finally, they should be created on the back of a 'facts and data' orientation—data on what is considered best in class, data on what competitors are doing, etc. The acronym is SPIF (stretch, predictability, improvement orientation, and facts and data)

Goals should address the needs and pains of customers, employees, investors and other stakeholders. An understanding of stakeholders and their needs is important. Similarly, goals should simultaneously address growth, efficiency and foundation-building. It can never be one at the cost of the other. During the time of growth, you cannot ignore efficiency or vice versa, and foundation-building is never passé. Foundation-building helps the company stay anchored and not get swept away by the winds as it scales. Foundation-building could be about creating mechanisms to ensure compliance with various laws and statutes that govern the business or defining and adhering to processes that ensure customer delight (even though it may slow things down a bit) or creating and strictly implementing a policy for prevention of harassment or creating and communicating a code of conduct and framework of governance. It could also be about investing in the right tools that enhance productivity and data security.

'Line of sight' is another important aspect of goal-setting. You cannot hold a person accountable for something she has no control over. Having said that, one needs to recognize that there are clear shades of grey here. First of all, no one has complete control on anything that matters, and what is in someone's control is debatable. Individuals who tend to take ownership believe that a lot more is under their control than those who shrug off ownership. Therefore, this is a bit of a grey area. A lot of things that may come across as something beyond an individual's control will, if you probe sufficiently, emerge as being at least partially under the control of the individual. Going to either extreme does not work. Some managers are very reluctant to set goals that are not completely in the line of sight because they worry about dealing with the argument: 'But I don't control this.' Such managers end up setting goals that are easy to achieve and do not stretch their team members. On the other hand, some managers set goals for their team members that are not in the line of sight, without paying attention to how they would achieve them or what support they may need. Such managers are either being naive or are trying to make their own lives easy by passing the buck down.

And finally, creating a culture of high performance is about managing talent. It is about identifying and classifying people systematically and driving actions based on this classification. We have found a simple nine-blocker based on the 'performance–potential' combination.

Map Individuals to a 'Nine-Blocker' based on 'Performance' and 'Potential'

Potential	Low Performance	Medium Performance	High Performance
High	**Block 3** Low on performance but have the potential to deliver better performance	**Block 2** Can get into Block 1 by demonstrating a higher level of performance	**Block 1** Exceptional with regards to demonstrated potential, performance and can be developed for future positions at an accelerated speed
Med	**Block 4** Low on performance but have the potential to deliver better performance	**Block 5** Strength and backbone of the organization's success	**Block 6** Can get into Block 1 by demonstrating a higher level of leadership potential
Low	**Block 9** Need support to contribute to an expected level. Monitor performance closely	**Block 8** Strength and backbone of the organization's success	**Block 7** Strength and backbone of the organization's success

Performance (Low — Medium — High)

Take Specific Actions Based on This

Potential	Low Performance	Medium Performance	High Performance
High	**Block 3** Give warning Provide coaching	**Block 2** Identify next development opportunity	**Block 1** Plan multiple moves
Med	**Block 4** Provide coaching Consider if in appropriate job or with appropriate manager	**Block 5** Enrich job	**Block 6** Identify next development opportunity
Low	**Block 9** Initiate Performance Improvement Plan	**Block 8** Enrich job	**Block 7** Enrich job

Performance (Low — Medium — High)

Dealing with Underperformers

Paul Spiegelman, the chief culture officer of Stericycle, a company that specializes in collecting and disposing regulated substances, such as medical waste, and providing services for recalled and expired goods, wrote an article in *Inc.* magazine titled 'Why You Need to Fire Bad Employees Right Now'.

Sometimes you encounter a situation where you see improvement after providing feedback but as soon as you take your eyes off, the employee seems to regress. This is something you need to be careful about. Individuals who are clear underperformers are relatively easy to spot and deal with. The ones who are on the cusp can undermine your scale journey because you are not sure if they would shape up eventually or would forever continue to be a drag. And you tend to be so occupied that you don't even get to see the damage they are causing.

There is one simple tip that always works, and like anything that always works, it is not easy to practise—don't take your eyes off such individuals, especially if they report to you or are in key roles even two levels below you. Keep them on your radar till you take a decision, one way or the other. In our experience, a lot of those on the cusp do not eventually work out, with the exception of a few. Every time you see an improvement after feedback, you hope that the change is for good, but a little later you are again faced with the same issue. This slows you down, takes away your personal time and creates frustration. So, you need to take quick calls in such cases. Take your eyes off an individual only if you believe that she is completely on automatic pilot both in terms of performance and work ethic.

The other common question that managers face in rapidly scaling start-ups is whether to put underperformers on a formal performance improvement plan (PIP). Organizations have put together this process to ensure fairness and prevent cowboy-style managers perpetuating a hire and fire culture. We have seen several situations where a manager does not communicate expectations clearly and does not take the time to review and provide feedback. As a result, there is a perception of underperformance. Initiating a separation based on such perceptions, without the manager doing her part well, sets off a culture of hiring and firing. Treat a PIP as a test condition where you have taken care to clearly define expectations and observe the individual closely. If your feedback and review mechanisms are perfect then the need for a formal PIP is minimal. We have seen some seasoned managers pulling off separations without a PIP just because at every stage they did what they were supposed to do—setting expectations clearly, periodically reviewing these and providing candid feedback.

Handling Exits Amicably Is Critical

Handling exits amicably could determine how the talent market views your company. Some managers don't seem to know how to do this. Once you have taken a decision to let go of an individual, be swift. Do not procrastinate and delay the difficult conversation. Be polite but firm. Do not get into arguments. Own the decision as the manager and agree on the next steps and timelines.

Do not stop treating the separating employees with respect and do not stop acknowledging they exist. If you suspect there is more harm in allowing them to stay and help with the transition, have a quick and clinical separation. If you have decided to let the person stay and help with the transition, don't treat her as persona non grata. Do not insist on her serving the notice period if there is no real need. Don't do this just to make life difficult for her or the company she is joining.

Maintain confidentiality. Someone once came up and asked, 'I am getting a lot of questions on XYZ's exit. Can we know the reasons?' Or a senior manager might come up and inquire about a colleague's separation, saying, 'I am not keen to know why, but my team members are asking me questions. What do I tell them?' In such situations, set the basic behaviour expectations right with seniors. They cannot be allowed to palm off their personal curiosity as questions from their teams. Read them the riot act on how to contain curiosity about other people's compensation, reasons for other people's separations, etc. Another common question is, 'We are letting the person go on performance (or integrity) grounds. Shouldn't we let people in the company know about that?' No way. This is not done. It can have serious legal and moral implications.

How you treat a separating employee has a huge impact on what the others think of you and what they can expect when they move. Treating separating employees with dignity, by acknowledging their right to separate without unnecessary discussion on their perceived opinions about the organization, is a critical component of a good culture. Some organizations have a terrible reputation when it comes to dealing with separating employees, and such organizations generally have low employee morale, and good people are reluctant to join them. Separated employees are some of your best brand ambassadors.

Cultivate and Nurture Good Feedback Mechanisms

You need to make feedback a way of life. Our basic philosophy in life is—say it if you like it and say it if you don't like it. Having said that, it is very important that you communicate what you don't like without getting personal. That is a bit of an art one needs to learn. You should create a totally apolitical and transparent climate, so that the candour is taken in the right spirit. Most people find it difficult to provide feedback because of one or more of the following reasons: a) they worry that the other person won't like them and it would be difficult to work with them after that, or that they'll end up hurting the other person's feelings; b) they fear that they would get a mouthful in return; or c) they have had previous experiences in which the receiver didn't change or became hostile.

In all these cases, they just may not have the skills to provide feedback and as a result worry about mishandling it. Feedback should be an easy and effortless process. Every feedback does not need a formal setting nor does it need to always be scheduled. Feedback works best when it's an ongoing process and is accepted as part of your team's routine. Feedback should never be sugar-coated. Don't get taken in too much by the HR and training folks who may suggest using a 'sandwich technique'. This technique is for beginners. Just take care that the feedback does not come across as personal. Feedback should be so unambiguous that it must result in only one of the two things: a) change; b) an acknowledgement from the recipient that she needs help in making the change. If it doesn't achieve one of these two outcomes quickly, then there is a flaw in the way feedback is provided.

In an ideal world, feedback should be substantiated by data; and, in an ideal world, negative feedback is better given in private. But there is nothing like an ideal world. Don't let these broad principles of an ideal world paralyse your actions in the real world you live in. It is actually very helpful sometimes to provide negative feedback in a public or at least a semi-public setting (a review with the team can be a semi-public setting)! You can get across messages very effectively. Just be careful that you don't take this to an extreme, where you are seen to be totally anecdotal or seen as callous or insulting.

Feedback needs an open mind (on your behalf). Be open to changing your position based on what you hear. An ability to change your position and acknowledge you were wrong can strengthen your reputation and make people even more open to feedback from you.

Customize your style. Identify your team members and mentally categorize them as 'reds', 'yellows' and 'greens' based on their ability to assimilate and act on feedback. Greens being the best and reds being the worst. With a green, you can be gentle and refined. For example, 'I have received this escalation. Take a look and get it fixed.' You can then casually check on the status in some time. With a yellow, you can be more firm and specific. For example, 'This has been escalated to me. This is serious nonconformity. Fix it and get back to me.' Plan to meet after a week to check on the status. With a red, you could be curt and explicit. For example, 'Meet me with a solution. And an explanation why this has happened.' Plan to meet the next day to check on the progress.

Incentive Plans, the Panacea for Everything . . . or Are They?

The power of incentive plans in driving desired outcomes is highly exaggerated. We have often come across statements like: 'Our incentive plan is not driving the right behaviours', 'Our sales staff doesn't believe this incentive plan can help us meet next year's stiff targets', or 'Our operations teams need to be incented to drive account growth'. We are quite surprised to see so many managers who seem to believe that incentive plans are an easy way to fix a problem irrespective of its nature.

Our experience in implementing incentive plans leads us to believe that most real problems cannot be solved by an incentive plan. However, there are some situations where a good solution can be cemented by a well-designed incentive plan. Incentive plans work best when outcomes can be directly linked to an individual's efforts. Small and self-sufficient teams with clearly defined goals, which are largely under their control, can also be motivated by incentive plans. In such cases, the incentive needs to be a significant component of their earnings. If the incentive is a miniscule part of their total compensation, it is unlikely to drive performance. Every individual makes an unconscious trade-off on the effort needed to achieve a stretch goal and the additional incentive that achieving the stretch goal would result in. If the incentive is a small component of the total earnings, the trade-off easily tips in favour of taking it easy and not putting in the kind of effort needed to achieve the stretch goal.

If leaders need to drive desired outcomes, they should stay focused on problem-solving, conducting better reviews, having difficult conversations, coaching their teams, communicating expectations or just providing direction. Using well-designed incentive plans to drive performance is not such a bad thing, especially in some contexts, but using incentive plans blindly to compensate for fundamental management failures can be fatal.

In Conclusion

The human capital tends to be a bit complex because of the number of variables and unavailability of a standard set of frameworks that can be applied to a situation. Each situation is extremely nuanced. However, at one level this is all common sense that can be honed with some effort.

We believe that of all the drivers of scale this is the most powerful because the underpinning of success of any other driver of scale is eventually a people issue. If you get the people equation right, the other things will line up eventually.

9

Inflection Points and Pivots

I found that every single successful person I've spoken to has had a turning point and the turning point was where they made a clear, specific, unequivocal decision that they were not going to live like this any more. Some people make that decision at fifteen and some people make it at fifty and most never make it at all.

—Brian Tracy, an American-Canadian motivational speaker

This applies as much to start-ups and companies as it does to individuals.

There is a lot common between the evolution of organisms and the evolution of organizations. They both go through the inexorable cycle of innovation, growth and decline. Decline in an organism can sometimes be arrested through timely mutations in which it develops traits that help deal with the adverse factors. These factors could either be internal or external. Similarly, organizations too can extend their decline through a new wave of innovation. This is not easy for several reasons.

Stories of Successful Pivots

Deep Kalra, the founder-CEO of MakeMyTrip (MMT), told us that MMT went through two major inflection points in its journey. MMT started off with selling air tickets on its platform. Air ticketing was a commodity business. The number of suppliers were limited (airlines), and they had their own distribution capabilities. They did not value MMT's distribution capability enough to part with sufficient margin. If there had been twenty airlines in the fray, the bargaining power of a platform like MMT would have automatically been strengthened from this competitive intensity. MMT wasn't making money.

However, the air ticketing business helped MMT build a large subscriber base. All of digital India that was travelling was on their platform. It became easy for MMT to pivot at this stage and move into hotels. This was a highly disaggregated category and a perfect market for a platform. Hotels were willing to part with significant margins in exchange for business. The obvious question is: Did this constitute a pivot or was it just about tapping an adjacent market using their same core capability? It was clearly an inflection point because hotels soon constituted a lion's share of the business. MMT went on to grow rapidly in value and hit a market capitalization in excess of $2 billion, while Yatra remained a sub $300 million company. If you can alter the trajectory of your business by moving to an adjacent segment (either customers or supply) that is fundamentally different from your current segment, then this move is a pivot. Another obvious question is: Why didn't Yatra just follow suit? Unlike the air ticketing business which was entirely technology-driven, the hotel business involved friction on the ground and needed a team with a different set of capabilities. MMT recognized this and built this capability quickly. Further, tech integration with four to five airlines was simple. Tech integration with thousands of hotels was a different kettle of fish altogether. Network effect soon kicked in, and hotels wanted to be on the MMT platform because travellers were on the platform, and vice versa.

Sometime in January 2017, in one of the biggest M&A deals in India, MMT acquired Ibibo. With this transaction, all the important brands in the consumer travel space—MMT, Goibibo, Redbus, Ryde and Rightstay—in India came under the umbrella of MMT. This was another major inflection point in MMT's journey. The big players who, prior to this deal were bleeding red ink in their financial statements, were able to successfully cut cash burn. This deal propelled MMT to the next orbit.

In another example, Daksh started off with providing outsourced email customer support. We had serious doubts about the willingness of American companies to take the risk of moving voice-based support to a country with a totally different accent. It was difficult to fathom that training could work wonders, and Nandini could be trained to speak like Nancy! However, the reality turned out to be different. Email support was not as ubiquitous as we thought it would become, and American companies demonstrated an appetite for outsourcing voice-based support to India. We soon pivoted to providing voice-based customer support. This called for a totally different capability and the execution was very challenging, but we built that capability. Starting from a niche market, we pivoted to tap into a much bigger and growing market.

WhatsApp, which started off by leveraging Apple's push notification feature to update 'status-tracking', soon pivoted to become an Internet-based messaging app. Jan Koum, the co-founder and CEO of WhatsApp, kept an inspirational note, given by his co-founder Brian Acton, always taped to his desk. It read: 'No Ads! No Games! No Gimmicks!' WhatsApp has stuck to this promise and continues to reject the idea of showing ads to its users. This promise has helped WhatsApp emerge as the winner over all other messaging apps offered by much bigger players.

Amazon and Myntra too pivoted successfully— Amazon from being an online book store to an 'everything store'; and Myntra from being an online store for 'gifting items' to an e-commerce site for fashion.

Another example of a successful pivot is the one UnitedLex made. UnitedLex is a unicorn in the technology and legal services space. They were focused on providing 'contract management' services. They soon discovered that the buyers of this service were spread within a large corporation, and therefore it involved selling the same thing to multiple small stakeholders within every corporation. On the other hand, they figured out that when it came to 'litigation services' the buying was centralized within a corporation and hence involved one strategic sale. Soon, UnitedLex learnt to focus on and build capability in this new sub-vertical of litigation within the broader vertical of legal, and this launched UnitedLex on to a new growth trajectory.

All these are examples of start-ups that attained significant scale. On the other hand, 'Rocketium', a modular platform with reusable Lego-like components—creative production, digital asset management, brand management, collaboration, workflow, analytics and process automation—is an example of an early-stage start-up that made a few significant pivots to discover the near-perfect product–market fit. We asked Satej Sirur, the founder-CEO of Rocketium, what product–market fit really meant to him. He says this is bit of a nebulous concept, but you can be sure of a good product–market fit if you see some of these signals: a) prospects or customers begin chasing you for meetings and product demos instead of you chasing them; b) customers asking you for new features with a sense of urgency or wanting to close deals quickly; c) you no longer have to sell a lot and instead are flooded with inbound interest; d) customers instantly connect with what you have to offer. It is evident that they are not being polite and nice. Their expression is one of 'Why didn't we know earlier that you existed?' He gives an example of a call with a senior executive at a Fortune 50 retail company in the US, where this executive spent the first ten minutes describing how it took twenty days to take a banner live. He concluded by saying that he was looking for this fictional product that could cut this time significantly. He spent the next twenty minutes watching his fictional product turn into reality when Rocketium's vice president, sales, walked him through how the Rocketium product would work on his company's platform. After fifteen seconds of pregnant silence, the executive just said, 'Why didn't we know earlier that you existed?!'

Rocketium made two pivots along the way, but the fundamental premise on which the platform was built remained unchanged—'people have short attention spans and engage with visuals better than with text or static imagery'. Starting from easy online creation of videos, with a feature-rich product and excellent support, Rocketium eventually pivoted to deliver products that integrated deeply into the workflow of their clients and helped them maximize their revenue through an in-app advertising solution. This brings us to an essential component of a pivot—it is a change in direction that addresses a different customer segment or solves a different problem. However, the underlying core capabilities and principles should drive the pivot. If you need to change everything you did before the pivot, including the core premise or capabilities on which the company was built, then you might as well shut and start a new company.

Rob Fitzpatrick, a YCombinator alumnus who has built products used globally by brands like MTV and Sony, in his book, *The Mom Test—How to Talk to Customers and Learn if Your Business Is a Good Idea When Everyone Is Lying to You*, says most founders either use overly opinionated questions like 'Do you think it's a good idea?', or very broad questions like 'Do you think there is a need for a product like this in the market?'. These questions result in an incorrect understanding about the market. He says, 'Asking your mother if she thinks your product is a good idea will always lead to a "yes". Unfortunately, your mother is not a real market.' The book is all about asking the right set of questions (for example, 'Talk Me Through the Last Time That Happened') that would help you truly figure out what you need to build, which is getting your product–market fit right. Frankly neither of us has read this book, but it has come up in numerous conversations with entrepreneurs who swear by it and believe that the examples of good and bad approaches illustrated in the book are very helpful in validating start-up ideas.

Paytm's Pivots Are Interesting and Intriguing

Paytm was founded in 2001 and offered live astrology advice for a telecom services provider. At that point of time, it wasn't known by the name Paytm. Very quickly it got into providing value-added services like gaming and subscription-based content. Vijay Shekhar Sharma recognized the future of mobiles in India early on and broadly stayed with the belief that this opportunity was huge and needed to be tapped. Almost every single pivot that Paytm made continued to leverage the ubiquitous presence and power of cell phones. Paytm as an entity came into being sometime in 2010 as an online recharge portal.

Sumit Chakraberty, then a journalist at Tech in Asia and now a consulting editor at *Mint*, published an article on Tech In Asia titled 'Paytm founder prepares for his next pivot, which could be the biggest yet'. In that he wrote, 'Paytm has earned a series of labels over the years: from SMS services to phone top-ups to a mobile commerce and fintech company. Vijay now simply calls it a mobile internet business as possibilities have exploded over the past couple of years, especially after the investment by Alibaba.'

Sometime in January 2014, the Nachiket Mor Committee on Comprehensive Financial Services for Small Businesses and Low Income Households, formed by the RBI, in its report recommended the formation of a new category of bank called payments bank. The primary purpose of this was to create no-frills banks that would increase financial inclusion by offering small savings accounts and payment remittance services to low-income households, migrant labour workforce, small businesses, other unorganized sector entities and similar users. For Paytm, this was a natural extension of its core platform. It obtained the payments bank licence sometime in January 2017. The problem with the Paytm wallet was that one needed to constantly move money into it from a bank account. Paytm's payments bank would address this problem. Wallet payments could become that much more seamless and easy to use.

A month later, inspired by China's largest B2C online retail platform, Tmall, Paytm launched Paytm Mall. In early 2019, eBay bought a 5.6 per cent stake in Paytm Mall. This was quite an unnecessary pivot and was obvious even at that point of time and not just in hindsight. Very soon, there were problems. There was no way Paytm Mall could compete with the likes of Flipkart or Amazon who had paid undivided attention to this category of consumer Internet. Paytm Mall had to resort to rampant cashbacks and discounts to win market share, which was not sustainable. It evaporated as soon as the cashbacks and discounts disappeared. After the mounting losses and being unable to make any headway, Paytm Mall shut down warehouses across many cities and migrated to an asset-light marketplace model.

While some of the pivots were opportunistic and smart, some of them came across as reckless and brash—the kind one makes when one is sitting on a huge pile of cash. As a result, Paytm became 'everything for everyone'. It remains to be seen how the company reinvents itself and manages its valuations in the future.

Why Do Companies Hit Inflection Points?

As companies grow bigger, they begin to add layers. These layers become more distant from the ground and slowly begin to get cut off from customer pain points, and tend to overlook underserved markets or unhappy customers. Individuals closer to the ground are often the most junior and least influential. It is not very easy to create 'listening' mechanisms that cut through hierarchy and ego. We mentioned in one of the earlier chapters that as start-ups grow, they need to institute stabilizing mechanisms to avoid destruction due to centrifugal forces. As a result, they lose some of the innovation zing. Eventually, despite its best efforts, the stabilizing forces begin to dominate and lead it towards a decline. Decision-making becomes excruciatingly slow. Organization structures become exceedingly complex and cumbersome. Structures become complex matrices with conflicting pulls and pressures, and the number of committees begins to grow in number. Skills that help navigate through organizational power structures become far more valued and important than clear thinking and understanding customer problems. It is far easier to be a naysayer in a large organization than to take risks. In smaller start-ups, the decision-making is like lightning. A decision to act on customer feedback by adding new features or even launching a new product can be taken in a matter of days or even hours. This might routinely take months and even years in large companies. Therefore, newer start-ups can identify customer segments or markets that are underserved by large incumbents and quickly fill the gaps before these incumbents can even recognize the intrusion. Large incumbents may even demonstrate arrogance by acting as if these little niches that they have left vacant are not worth their time and attention. Before long the niches expand and can become mainstream.

Success and market clout also bring in the inevitable complacence, arrogance and hubris. We believe complacence is a deeply wired outcome of success which is an essential part of the corporate cycle of birth, death and regeneration. Speed, closeness to customers, feedback mechanisms and execution, which are the building blocks of entrepreneurial energy, get diluted with time.

The tech industry is full of examples where giant incumbents have been outsmarted by more nimble and young start-ups. Nobody ever thought that the dominance of Nokia or BlackBerry could ever be challenged. Nokia was the undisputed leader in the mobile handset market and BlackBerry was the leader when it came to corporate email. Both were totally obliterated in a very short span of time by Apple. From undisputed market leadership to total annihilation, the journey was swift. Dell came from behind and displaced the IBM PC. It displaced Compaq and HP as well. The tech industry is full of such cases. Facebook will not be displaced by another giant. In all likelihood, the company that displaces Facebook will be birthed in a garage, or a dorm at MIT or IIT.

In e-commerce, start-ups operating in smaller verticals (around say grocery, furniture, eye care, pharma, etc.) have built successful businesses (BigBasket, Pepperfry, Lenskart, PharmEasy). On paper, the e-commerce companies with a horizontal play like Flipkart and Amazon were much better funded but have struggled to compete with these verticals. Creating a razor-sharp focus around each of these verticals within a horizontal e-commerce company has proven to be far more difficult than imagined earlier. The broader point is that just because a large incumbent is well-resourced, it does not mean smaller niche players cannot outfox it. 'Bounce', an Indian start-up built around providing bikes that can be unlocked through an app for last-mile connectivity in urban commute, has been able to build a successful business through focus. Despite being much better funded, Ola could not prevent 'Bounce' from building this business. Therefore, an agile start-up can compete effectively against a giant incumbent through better focus. The giant incumbents need to use managers to build these new niches, while the upstarts bring much superior entrepreneurial energy. For this very reason, start-ups like Ola and Flipkart successfully challenged Uber and Amazon in India because the latter were just outposts of Uber US and Amazon US.

Pivots and Inflection Points at Large Companies

Someone once remarked that IBM had more committees than the Government of the United States. Despite all the criticism of moving at the pace of an elephant, IBM has been successful at navigating the inflection points in its journey with panache. As a result, it has continued to remain relevant even after a century.

In the 1970s, IBM dominance in the mainframe market was total. The acronym BUNCH was the nickname for the group of mainframe computer competitors to IBM in the 1970s. The name is derived from the names of five companies: Burroughs, UNIVAC, NCR, Control Data

Corporation (CDC) and Honeywell. These companies were grouped together because the market share of IBM was much higher than all of its competitors put together. During the 1960s, IBM and these five computer manufacturers, along with RCA and General Electric, were known as 'IBM and the Seven Dwarfs'. The description of IBM's competitors changed after GE's 1970 sale of its computer business to Honeywell and RCA's 1971 sale of its computer business to Sperry, leaving only five 'dwarves'. The companies' initials thus lent themselves to the acronym BUNCH.

Despite dominance in the mainframe market, IBM had no presence in the microcomputer market, which was small. However, by the 1970s, the market was slowly picking up, and by 1979 it was big enough to draw IBM's attention. The market was also projected to grow significantly. Realizing that it had no presence in a large and growing market, IBM decided to make a foray into this space despite internal scepticism and advice to stick to the knitting.

Some of the senior-most executives at IBM had the foresight to realize that over the years the organization had become too slow and bureaucratic. There was no way it could respond quickly with its own product. So, they made the bold move of relocating some of the best engineers to Boca Raton in Florida and insulated this team from the rest of IBM. This team had special budgets, could break the rules and was provided access to the senior-most decision-makers. Very soon, the IBM PC was launched. It went on to become a grand success. The BUNCH companies would follow IBM into the microcomputer market in the 1980s with their own PC compatibles.

Lockheed Corporation created Skunk Works to overcome the challenge of innovating in the context of a large corporation. The growing threat of German air power during World War II forced the US to quickly develop a fighter jet of its own. The US Air Force met with Lockheed Aircraft Corporation to develop an airframe around the most powerful jet engine that the allied forces had access to, the British Goblin. Lockheed was chosen to develop the jet because of its past interest in jet development and its previous contracts with the air force. One month after the meeting, a team of young engineers at Lockheed delivered the proposal to the air force. Two days later, the go-ahead was given to Lockheed to start development and Skunk Works was born, with Kelly Johnson at the helm.

The formal contract for the airframe did not arrive at Lockheed until four months after the work had already begun. This would prove to be a common practice in Skunk Works. Many times a customer would come to Skunk Works with a request, and on a handshake the project would begin, without any contracts or official submittal process. Kelly Johnson and his Skunk Works team designed and built the airframe in only 143 days, seven fewer than was required.

Skunk Works ran like IBM's PC project: It cut through the red tape of rules and procedures of the parent.

Smart companies try to delay the descent into bureaucracy by staying agile (or pretending to) and sensitive to customer needs. Smart companies also use the Skunk Works approach and once in a while bounce back to a new cycle of innovation. But the energy of youth and the inevitability of death often result in a small start-up with a young founder eventually disrupting this behemoth.

External factors can accelerate the arrival of an inflection point and accentuate its impact if it is already grappling with internal challenges. External factors could be a recession, a new invention, a regulatory upheaval or a host of others.

If companies are cognizant of the fact that it becomes increasingly difficult for large companies to innovate, they try and acquire promising start-ups and provide them with autonomy and support. Acquisitions may or may not work out. The reality is that half of the acquisitions end up as total failures. Half the mergers fail because of a) culture incompatibility; b) overestimating synergies and benefits at the time of the acquisition that do not eventually materialize on the ground; and c) integrating too quickly.

The trick is to make the other half work. Facebook recognized that the younger generation no longer considered Facebook cool and trendy and hence moved swiftly to acquire Instagram and WhatsApp. Companies like IBM have mastered the art and science of integrating companies they acquire. In one of the biggest acquisitions, IBM acquired PwC Consulting, the global management consulting and technology services unit of PricewaterhouseCoopers in October 2002. The deal was valued at approximately $3.5 billion in cash and stock. Some of the other more well-known acquisitions by IBM were Lotus Development Corporation and Tivoli. In the first ten years of this century itself, IBM acquired an average of nine companies a year! These acquisitions have helped IBM in no small measure to stay at the cutting edge.

To deal with the risk of failed integrations, companies have now begun to incubate and accelerate their own set of start-ups. For example, Shell Corporation's technology centre in Bengaluru has been incubating energy-related start-ups, and banks in India have begun incubating and accelerating fintech start-ups. Incubators and accelerators seem to be the new mantra in the start-up world.

The cycle of innovation, growth and decline is universally represented as an 'S' curve. The 'S' curve, like the Pareto principle, is a somewhat universal principle that finds application across a wide spectrum of disciplines. The 'S' curve represents the lifecycle of an innovation, namely, an early stage of resistance to change because of entrenched ideas and interests, followed by a stage of rapid growth when the benefits of the new idea become too obvious and enormous to be ignored, culminating in the idea being replaced by another innovation—the eternal cycle of birth, growth and death.

In Conclusion

After researching thirty-nine unicorns in the US, Aileen Lee in the same article in TechCrunch concluded among other things that, 'the "big pivot" after starting with a different initial product is an outlier'. Steve Blank, a Silicon Valley entrepreneur, in an article in *Entrepreneur* magazine a couple of months after Aileen Lee's article on TechCrunch, disagreed with this conclusion and claimed that Lee had viewed a pivot from a very narrow lens. To Lee's credit, she had qualified the word pivot with 'big'.

Watching my (Hari) daughter play basketball is sheer joy. Her grace is utterly mesmerizing. When I was once driving her back home after a big game, I asked her what pivoting in basketball meant. No one had ever asked her this question before. She reflected on this for a few seconds and explained that in a pivot, one foot is firmly on the ground and the other is used to re-position for a pass or a shot in a way that avoids a defensive player. I'm not sure I understood this fully in the basketball context, but it was clear that an analogy in the start-up world would be to stick to some of your core ideas, or foundation, and make changes to some component of your business model in a manner that would suddenly put you back in the game or take you to a higher orbit by creating a better product–market fit or sharper differentiation for your product.

The right pivots are helpful. No one gets their act right from the word go. A start-up always begins with a set of hypothesis that it is constantly trying to validate. When the traction is insufficient, it is time to question a few things with an open mind. Hanging on to an idea because you always felt strongly about it in the face of evidence to the contrary is not right. At the same time, losing your head and forgetting that an important component of a pivot is that one foot needs to be steady and firm is damaging.

10

Foundation: Technology, Process and Training

If you can't describe what you are doing as a process, you don't know what you are doing.

—Edwards Deming, American engineer
and statistician

During my days at Virtusa, I used to visit Boston often. During these visits, what never ceased to surprise me was how even in the middle of the night in some sleepy suburb, where the traffic was minimal, the cars would come to a complete halt when the traffic signal turned red. This contrasted with the chaos at traffic signals in Indian cities. How could human beings in one part of the world behave so differently from those in a different part? And why did Indians, who behaved in a certain way in their own country, suddenly start behaving differently when they moved to America? And that too with regard to something as simple as adherence to traffic rules! We will come to this shortly, but first a story on how we achieved such fundamental behavioural transformation in the context of a rapidly scaling start-up.

BigBasket does home delivery of groceries. The assortment was huge, nearly 40,000 SKUs (stock-keeping units), ranging from fast-moving consumer goods (FMCG), fruits and vegetables (F&V), chilled and frozen items (C&F), and more. There were some aspects of customer experience that were broken at some point of time, but we will talk of three specific examples and how we fixed them.

The C&F items were packed in chiller boxes, with frozen gel packs inside, to maintain the desired temperature. The delivery staff would often open up the chiller boxes and move stuff from one box to the other to minimize the number of boxes they had to lug around, even though they had been told this was a process violation. This would result in deterioration of the product quality because of temperatures exceeding the safe limits.

Now the second example. Grocery items were all packed in crates to prevent items getting messed up and mixed up. You couldn't pack toilet cleaners with food items, for instance. So each category of products was delivered in crates with different colours. And each crate was sealed with finely ribbed plastic cords similar to what some airlines use for sealing baggage. Before departing from the hub, for making deliveries, every delivery boy had to wrap a pouch around his waist. The pouch had a small cutter, among other things, which had to be used to cut the plastic cords from the crates. These had to be put back into the crates and not discarded at the customer's premises. The delivery staff almost never carried the cutter and simply ripped open the crate covers. In the process, they ended up damaging the crates, dropping the plastic cords on the floor and creating a shoddy experience for customers.

Now the final example. In the early stages of growth, most of the training of the delivery staff happened through a buddy mechanism, where a senior delivery executive trained a newly hired delivery executive and a senior warehouse executive trained a newly hired warehouse executive. Process updates were not reliably disseminated, and basic soft skills like greeting a customer, dealing with women and senior citizens were imparted inconsistently. This approach had worked reasonably well at the scale that BigBasket had operated on until then. But gradually the cracks were beginning to show: customer complaints were on the rise, productivity was low, and deliveries did not match invoices, among others. And BigBasket was growing rapidly. There were plans to hire another 6000 associates in the next twelve months.

What we needed was a 'six sigma' kind of precision in the way these processes worked on the ground.

Processes Work Only if They Are Followed Every Time

Nothing better fits the description of a double-edged sword as 'processes'. Processes can slow you down, but also help you scale without the wheels coming off. Processes can be stifling, but can be liberating in the sense that you don't have to worry whether something will get done the way you want it to. Processes can slow down and even frustrate a bright and smart individual, but even average individuals can deliver an outstanding experience every time if backed by them. And scale is all about getting average individuals to deliver outstanding experiences.

But we soon recognized that the unpleasant and inglorious side of processes was that even the average individuals who could benefit from this, hesitated to follow them if they slowed them down or made them work harder.

So, we added three additional layers to make these processes work every time, namely, audit, training and technology.

It is normal human tendency to circumvent a difficult process when there are no consequences. We quickly put together strong audit mechanisms to ensure that what was prescribed in the manual was actually delivered on the ground. Game theory explains several phenomena beautifully—why individuals collaborate and work well in cross-functional teams in some companies and why they fail miserably in some other companies; why traffic rules are followed in some countries and why they are regularly breached in some other countries. In countries and companies where processes work, the penalty for not demonstrating the desired behaviours or committing process breaches is so high that they tilt the scales heavily in favour of compliance.

We strengthened training. We helped the delivery executives understand the consequences of breaching some of these key processes. Most individuals demonstrate change when they fully comprehend the consequences of their current actions. Operations felt that the current method of using senior role holders to train the new joiners worked well because no time was wasted in training. But we changed that and introduced role-based training with good content and delivery mechanisms. We even introduced a process for trainer certification that ensured every single trainer conducted the training in exactly the same way.

We also took the call of soliciting feedback from customers on our delivery executives through push notifications. Feedback was categorized under a few heads, and there was space for some free text as well. With the help of our analytics team, we parsed through reams of free text to understand the overall customer sentiment and other behavioural issues with our delivery staff. With timely feedback, some of the behavioural issues vanished overnight. Based on the feedback, we identified the bottom 30 per cent every month. These individuals, with special focus on the bottom 10 per cent, were put through intense refresher training. The top 10 per cent were invited to come to some of these refresher sessions and talk about what they did differently. A simple Pareto showed that 10 per cent of the delivery staff was contributing to 70 per cent of the problems. With this data we could target improvement programmes that gave us bang for our training buck.

Continuous refresher training became a way of life. As some wise man or woman had once said, 'Sixty years ago I knew everything; now I know nothing; education is a progressive discovery of our own ignorance.' One could say the same thing about training as much as education. Any process is as good as the person behind it. And any person is as good as the training she has been through.

And finally, we brought in technology. All the chiller boxes were equipped with Internet of Things (IoT) devices. These could track the temperature from the hub, where the products were placed in these boxes, right until they were delivered to the customers. A dashboard was available to the operations controller at the hub who could then monitor the temperature of every chiller box that was dispatched. Any process deviation was detected and corrective actions were initiated immediately.

Technology, training and audit together ensured that process adherence became the norm.

Technology Scaling and Debt

Rakshit Daga's career in SAP began with a role in the office of the CEO and one of its legendary founders, Hasso Plattner, at Palo Alto. He got to see from close quarters Plattner's evolving belief in building products that incorporated design thinking. The principles behind design thinking have been around for a while, and like most concepts and frameworks in management, it is old wine in a new bottle. Design thinking is a combination of going beyond self-imposed constraints and mental models on the one hand and a deep understanding of the users on the other. It has been known by various names in the past, 'thinking out of the box' and 'problem-solving' being some of them.

A few months into his new role, Rakshit was tasked with setting up a team within SAP Labs called AppHaus (house of apps) that would build apps on top of the SAP platform. AppHaus was set up to work like a start-up even though it was part of a global organization. A few months into this role, Rakshit's boss wanted to know if he would be interested in moving to Bengaluru to set up an AppHaus team in India. After some thought, Rakshit took on the challenge of moving himself and his family back to India. It seemed to be an opportune time to move to India both professionally and personally. Professionally, this was a great opportunity to manage a global team across India, China, US and Europe. Personally, it provided his kids the opportunity to study in India during their formative years, while also allowing Rakshit to be close to ageing parents.

The India that Rakshit came back to, after a decade in the US, was different from the country he had left. He observed that the India he was returning to was a resurgent economy characterized by a young population. Rakshit tried replicating the start-up culture of the US AppHaus in India as well and succeeded to a great extent.

Having seen both sides (Silicon Valley and India), he had some great insights to offer.

The average age of a developer in India is around twenty-five years, and in Silicon Valley it is more like thirty-five. This is the genesis of some of the key differences in the software development practices between the Valley and India. While the work ethic of the engineers is India is second to none, this difference in the demographic profile of developers has generally led to some challenges.

'Technical Debt' is prevalent everywhere but it is much more accentuated in India. Technical debt (also known as tech debt or code debt) describes what happens when, in trying to expedite the delivery of a feature or functionality, development teams resort to shortcuts in terms of documentation and architecture that later need a lot of rework. This happens when speed to market is far more critical than good code.

In India there is a tendency to throw bright people at problems, including in the most successful start-ups.

In software development, there are often multiple ways of solving a problem, and mathematically smart people always find solutions. However, they have not yet been exposed to good architectural practices. As a result, they bring the product to market pretty quickly but incur a lot of technology debt in the process. In the Valley, because of more senior engineers in the team, the core infrastructure is created more thoughtfully, in a way that reduces technology debt and allows scaling to be more seamless. This is a result of their having solved complex problems earlier that gives them an innate sense of how architectural frameworks would scale in the long run. The interesting point is that the effort involved in getting the plumbing right at the very start does not really slow down development or delay the product launch. It is just that most young engineers simply do not know of the existence of these nuts and bolts.

For example, it takes a while for a young engineer to figure out that not all code needs to be synchronous. As software operations become large and complex, synchronous code becomes very slow and fragile to execute. Designing databases that can scale by minimizing computational load is another important component of scaling. These are practices that come with experience.

In India, the very successful IT services industry created managers out of engineers, and no engineer was keen to code after a certain point of time. Managing large teams was considered cool. As a result, there was a big gap in the availability of good software developers in the thirty-five–forty-year age bracket. While this is changing rapidly now, this resulted in the way software development was done at start-ups. Often, the first version of the product would be a prototype that would keep expanding in a random fashion because developers would keep building on top it. Add to this the poor quality of documentation and, after a while, no one knew how the code really worked. Since business was always growing rapidly, there was no time to think about the scalability challenge. Bright engineers were always busy solving problems around the same architecture and ended up with a system that consumed more energy, time and money to serve the same traffic. At some point, the burden of this technology debt begins to weigh heavily on performance, stability and scalability; and BigBasket was no exception to this piling up of technology debt.

In the last decade, there has been rapid development in technologies like virtualization and cloud computing that has made scaling far simpler. Fifteen years ago, if you had an e-commerce website that was expected to see a spike of say 10X in traffic because of a promotional sale or if you were an online video streaming platform and you expected a 100X spike because of a popular game, there was no way you could handle these peaks without a huge investment in large data centres. This investment would be underutilized after the spike disappeared. Today, developers need not worry about hardware limitations to the same extent, or for that matter plan a lot in advance.

In 1998, a personal computer with 512 MB RAM would have cost $700. Today a smartphone with twice the computing power comes at a fraction of this cost. This has provided every developer a strong client infrastructure that could be used to interface with large server systems powering the world's most common apps.

As start-ups scale, they need to rethink how they should organize their technology teams. The start-up culture of everyone pitching in and doing anything that needs to be done results in work being assigned based on bandwidth and not on expertise; it results in knowledge of any system being fragmented among team members. Hence, a dedicated 'platforms team' that acts as a single-point owner for the IT infrastructure becomes essential to deliver performance at scale. The architecture needs to be reconfigured to a micro-services model. This would help compartmentalize the code base and isolate the risk of performance issues to the specific micro-service rather than the entire codebase and data store. One needs to watch against bureaucracy at this stage because it could lower the average productivity of developers.

In Conclusion

Technology, process and training are three very powerful enablers of scale. As your start-up scales, you would need to hire people in the leadership team who understand these very well. The unstoppable march of technology has put immeasurable power in the hands of those who know how to harness it. Leadership teams and even individual leaders who do not recognize the power of technology and the strategic impact it can have on the business are doomed to be laggards.

Processes and training, as enablers of scale, have been enduring and timeless. However, their power is often underestimated because they tend to be a bit soft and intangible. Together with technology, they make a formidable combination that can power a start-up in the journey of scale.

11

Build to Sell or Build to Last

You should always run a company as if it will last forever. The best businesses are sellable—even if you have no intention of cashing out or stepping back anytime soon.

—John Warrillow, in *Built to Sell*

This binary choice or classification may or may not be appropriate. Start-ups can be founded and built with multiple motives, and the manner in which they evolve and eventually exit may or may not have anything to do with the initial intent of the founders.

In hindsight, it may appear that every large company that went on to list on a stock exchange or was acquired started off with a 'built to last' mindset. That may or may not be true.

One is also likely to assume that the probability of a start-up with a 'built to last' mindset doing a successful IPO is much higher than a 'built to sell' start-up. This assumption may not be true either, simply because it is extremely difficult to take a start-up to IPO even if it was built and run as if it would last forever. The probability of a death or acquisition is almost equally likely for both the categories.

Therefore, the final outcome (shutdown, acquisition, an IPO, or becoming an 'academy' company) does not always reflect the initial intent. However, our belief is that of the really few start-ups that eventually end up outliving their founders and becoming academy companies, almost all of them were founded on a 'built to last' mindset.

The 2x2 below is a good classification of those who build and/or run organizations:

		Weak	Strong
Passion for Creation	**Strong**	Incubators	Institution Builders
	Weak	Lead Small Teams (in Large Organizations)	Lead Large Organizations

Love for Scale and Complexity

Founders in the top left-hand corner are the 'incubators'. They love incubating new businesses. The motive for this may be twofold, namely, a) building a business around their passion; b) building opportunistically with an eye on selling it. Both may eventually end up selling unless circumstances conspire to keep the founder away from an exit.

Sudeep Kulkarni, co-founder of 'Tribe Fitness' and 'Game Theory', is deeply passionate about sports and fitness. Fitness was not such a cool thing in India until the beginning of this decade and wasn't something people liked to talk or brag about. Sticking to a fitness programme was one of the biggest challenges people faced. It usually remained one of the forgotten New Year's resolutions. Sudeep believed that if people could exercise in a group in a cool facility, fitness could become popular and even fashionable. It turned out exactly as they had envisioned. In 2017, Cure.fit acquired Tribe Fitness. It had acquired 'Cult', a similar start-up, a year back in 2016. The founders of Tribe Fitness and Cult were 'incubators'. They built their businesses around their passion. They were not the kind of entrepreneurs who loved running complex-scale businesses. Running a scale business needs a different set of skills and motives. They realized that the businesses they had built would scale better under the Cure.fit umbrella. So selling out and going on to pursue their next big dream was a natural choice. Sudeep is now busy building his next start-up, 'Game Theory', which is trying to bring sports closer to local neighbourhoods.

There also is a second category of 'incubators'.

In the first half of 2018, there was a spate of investments in hyperlocal milk delivery start-ups in India, such as Doodhwala, SuprDaily, DailyNinja, MilkBasket, Morning Cart, RainCan, among others. While some of them were into pure milk delivery, others quickly diversified to supply a few daily essentials along with milk. The value proposition was simply the convenience of being able to order at night through an app and having the stuff delivered at the doorstep the next morning.

This was a new service that no organized player had attempted before because of the obvious reason of awfully poor unit economics. The margins on milk were wafer-thin and could never cover the costs for an organized player. But this did not deter some of these start-ups that saw an opportunity to acquire users who would transact twenty-five times a month!

These were clearly businesses that were 'built to sell'. There were no defensible moats and the unit economics on a standalone basis were quite hopeless. It would be very easy for a well-capitalized and established player to bulldoze its way into this space unhindered, and walk away with their business. These start-ups wanted to rapidly scale this business under the radar and acquire a huge base of loyal customers before some of the big players took notice. At which point they would be ripe candidates for an acquisition.

But things changed rapidly on the ground. The burn rates for these start-ups continued to be high with no real possibility of improving unit economics. Funding dried up faster than anticipated. Bigger players like BigBasket acquired three of these players, Morning Cart, RainCan, and DailyNinja, and rapidly scaled the business. By increasing the variety of daily essentials that could be supplied along with milk, the unit economics suddenly turned around. All the other hyperlocal start-ups in this space have been in frantic talks with potential buyers.

While the 'build to sell' category of start-ups is easy to spot, there really is no 'build to last'.

No Intent Is Good or Bad

We believe that there are fundamentally two differences between a 'build to sell' approach and all other approaches. First, the stakeholders being addressed in each of these approaches are different. A 'build to sell' approach is about looking around to discover opportunities that would be interesting to the biggies in the market with deep pockets. These biggies could be large companies or private equity firms. In contrast, a 'build to last' approach is about looking for problems being faced by customers or enterprises and finding sustainable solutions for them. Second, the concept of 'founder–idea fit' is not there in a 'build to sell' approach, whereas founders who start with other intents are often passionate about the idea they pick to work on. Some of them do not have a penchant for running it beyond a point and actively scout out for a buyer, while others are happy to scale and grow the business without limits.

In the above example, the hyperlocal start-ups were clearly looking at the big daddies of e-commerce like Amazon, Flipkart, BigBasket or even food-tech companies like Swiggy and Zomato to buy them out. They knew that these biggies were focused on their core business and had no time to spare for these fringe categories. While these categories may not have made economic sense on a standalone basis, especially in a VC investing context, they would have made eminent sense as part of a broader range of offerings for a bigger e-commerce player. Therefore, if they could use this opportunity to rapidly build a business that would be a logical extension for these large companies at a later date, it would fetch them a good price. This could obviously backfire if the biggies chose to organically build this business when they could free themselves a bit.

The Decision to Sell or Continue to Operate

Based on extensive research over a ten-year period from 2003–13, Jason Rowley, a venture capital and technology reporter based in Chicago, in an article published on TechCrunch in 2017 titled 'Here's how likely your start-up is to get acquired at any stage', showed that of all the start-ups that found a successful exit, about 6 per cent were through an IPO and the balance 94 per cent were through an acquisition. It is very unlikely that the 94 per cent of start-ups began their journey with a 'build to sell' mindset. It just indicates that irrespective of the mindset, the reality is that a predominantly large percentage of start-ups end up getting acquired.

When I (Sanjeev) started Daksh, I strongly believed that we could be the Infosys of the business process outsourcing (BPO) space. For the few who may not know the Infosys analogy, it was one of India's most highly respected global companies built by a bunch of first-generation entrepreneurs whose families had no business background. They were bright engineers from India's premier educational institutions who decided to do something different and built one of India's most respected and values-driven company. Coming back to

Daksh, despite the crowded space, very soon it turned out to be a two-horse race—Daksh and Spectramind. Soon, Spectramind was acquired by Wipro. We hoped to continue to grow and go the IPO route. However, over a period of time, the business developed a client concentration. This is a pretty well-known business risk. It means a small number of clients contribute to a disproportionate chunk of the revenue. If the choice is between developing client concentration by accepting new business and avoiding the same by turning down this business, the decision is a no-brainer. You will accept the business any day as long as on a standalone basis it is of good quality. At Daksh, a US telecom major contributed to a large chunk of revenue. At that time, this telecom major was going through its own challenges in terms of how it was perceived by customers in relation to its major competitors. To make matters worse, there were a series of senior leadership exits. The company hired IBM Consulting to help them with a strategic plan to arrest their decline and reposition themselves as a reliable and customer-centric service provider. As part of the comprehensive consulting engagement, IBM figured out that it would be helpful to move the telecom major's customer contact centres from India to the Philippines. Philippines had been a US colony from 1898 to 1946, and the two countries had a lot of cultural similarities. Coupled with the availability of low-cost English-speaking resources—who spoke in an American accent— Philippines was fast emerging as a destination for customer service outsourcing for American companies. The icing on the cake was that Filipinos were known to be naturally customer-centric. So, when IBM made an offer to Daksh for an acquisition, we went ahead and signed the deal. After the acquisition, Daksh went on to build one of the biggest customer contact centres in Manila, under the IBM umbrella. Daksh, now a fully owned subsidiary of IBM, helped grow IBM's BPO business exponentially. Through their technology consulting services, IBM had built deep client relationships with most American corporates and this helped drive business for Daksh. Daksh no longer needed to go out and sell. IBM sales representatives from other lines of business, including consulting, were cross-selling BPO.

This brings us to an important lesson of whether to sell your business or continue to run it. You should continue to run your business if you believe you can run it better than anyone else in terms of operational rigour, growth, sales and distribution, and customer experience. You should be open to an acquisition if you believe the business can be better driven by being a part of a larger entity. The other reality check is that the odds of building an institution that outlasts you are very low, and you should deal with this with equanimity.

In another story, Uber chose to sell out to Didi Chuxing in China in 2016 after nearly three years of operations and realizing that all the odds were stacked against them, including the Chinese government's attitude to foreign companies operating in China. In return, Uber got a 20 per cent stake in Didi. By then, Uber had burnt through nearly $2 billion of cash. However, the decision to sell turned out to be a smart move. If they had continued, it would have meant even more cash burn. With Uber shutting, Didi became a monopoly with better control over pricing. Uber's stake in Didi some years later was valued at nearly $7 billion. There couldn't have been a better return on investment.

In another story, Virtusa listed on NASDAQ in 2007. Shortly, Metavante Technologies, a Wisconsin-based technology company that provided financial technology services, regulatory advice and consulting to its customers (consisting primarily of small- to large-sized financial institutions), reached out to Virtusa for an acquisition. It meant taking a public company back to being a private company again. At that point of time, the founder of Virtusa, Kris Canekeratne, had run it for nearly eleven years. Kris had always been of the view that one should run a company as if it was built to last and that an IPO was just another milestone. Though it is fashionable to say this, most founders run out of steam after an IPO and do not have the penchant for running a low-growth company in a predictable manner quarter after quarter.

There were terrific synergies between Virtusa and Metavante. Talks began in earnest. However, there was a black swan event in the form of the global credit crisis. Talking of black swans, we realized that they were not as rare as Nassim Taleb had made them out to be! Companies of all kinds were shaken up by the credit crisis and most plans went terribly awry. The talks were called off. Virtusa continued to be a public company and Kris continues to run it to this day. Along the way, it went on to reach a market capitalization of a billion dollars and more. This is a classic case of how difficult it is to plan an exit, and the value of John Warrillow's advice that one should always run a company as if it would last forever.

Window Dressing

Irrespective of whether it is a 'build to sell' or a 'build to last' case, it is not uncommon for start-ups contemplating an exit to do some window dressing. This is essentially trying to make your company look better than it actually is. In doing this, you are hoping that the buyer does not see through it and you can obtain a higher price. This is clearly not a good thing, but it is a bit of a grey area in the sense that looking better than you actually are through make-up has never been considered a bad thing unless one goes overboard. Buyers understand this well and hence go through every aspect of the business of a potential acquisition candidate with a fine-toothed comb.

Examples of window dressing include trying to boost profitability by deferring essential expenditure or by cutting essential expenditure. Deferring essential expenditure could include deferring licence renewals, putting a hold on hiring, postponing maintenance, etc. Some of the cuts may not show up adversely in the short term, and the hope is that the buyer won't see through this. Window dressing could also take the form of adding poor-quality customers or revenue, which could come in many forms. It could be revenue from customers with a high likelihood of default in payments or non-repeat revenue or revenue at low price points (and hence low margins).

It again boils down to the wisdom that it is always a good idea to continue to build the business as if it would last forever. Mathematicians say that lying is a wrong strategy from a game theory perspective, besides being morally reprehensible. Similarly, window dressing is a strategy that has a higher probability of hurting your business and personal reputation than doing any good, besides potentially depriving you of a good night's sleep.

In Conclusion

Businesses that are founded with a 'built to last' mindset have a greater probability of achieving long-term success and creating value for all the stakeholders. The founders and employees at such start-ups are more likely to be motivated and happy because they are working towards a mission. Deep inside there is a sense of self-respect and pride. The culture is more stimulating and the likelihood of recovering from lows is much higher. Having said this, as we illustrated earlier, the final outcome depends upon a host of factors, which are beyond the control of the founders or their investors.

12

Ten Good Habits

Your work is going to fill a large part of your life, and the only way to be truly satisfied is to do what you believe is great work. And the only way to do great work is to love what you do.

—Steve Jobs, co-founder, chairman and CEO, Apple

Rides to the Kempegowda airport, Bengaluru, to catch early-morning flights in winter are occasions to savour the uniquely refreshing and crisp air. One Saturday, I (Hari) left my house in the wee hours to catch a flight to Kochi. This was a journey I had waited for with bated breath for over two weeks.

Kochi was relatively warm and humid. After getting out of the airport, I boarded a cab to get to Ponnani, a small, nondescript village about three hours from Kochi by car. The directions were clear and I had no difficulty finding the place. The door was opened by the man himself.

The man I was meeting was none other than E. Sreedharan, recipient of the prestigious Padma Vibhushan and the Lifetime Achievement Award for Entrepreneurship by the *Economic Times*, among many others. At eighty-seven years of age, he has the energy and liveliness of a fifty-year-old. No wonder he is still consulted by governments and government institutions.

He was responsible for some of modern India's engineering marvels like the Konkan Railway and the Delhi Metro. Whenever he undertook projects of this magnitude, he did two things: a) hire a formidable start-up team; and b) create a great culture. Every member of the team had to have a demonstrated track record of execution and integrity. Large contracts were involved and even the slightest insinuation of corruption could derail the project. He was a magnet for talented engineers. Great founders have the same approach when they start companies. Every start-up now talks about culture, which is the biggest driver of performance whether the organization is a start-up or a large public institution. Sreedharan had the unique ability to transform the culture of a place wherever he went. The most striking case is what he did when he was deputed as the managing director of Cochin Shipyard. The relationship between the management and the unions was extremely confrontational. Corruption was rife. Through the correct use of the carrot-and-stick approach, he quickly transformed the culture. He had to face a lot of political pressure when the unions threatened to strike. However, Sreedharan stood his ground on the core issues. Finally, the unions were completely won over when they realized his true motives. Ironically, when he had to get back to the railways after turning around the shipyard, the unions at the shipyard did everything they could to stall the move!

When we subsequently reflected on this conversation, we realized that great entrepreneurs and institution builders have five common traits:

- They are all men and women of unquestionable integrity and competence.
- Personal aggrandizement is never a priority. Not even low down on the list.
- They all understand that nothing of significance, and scale is one such thing, can be ever built without taking your key stakeholders along with you.
- They realize that solving complex problems calls for tenacity, patience and risk-taking.
- They understand the difference between compromises that help in getting closures or speeding up implementation and compromises that jeopardize the basic objectives of an idea or a programme. They know when to be flexible and when to stand one's ground.

Are There Some Universally Good Habits for Scaling?

We talked of a playbook for scaling in chapter 2. If you are solving a niche problem, which is perfectly all right, then rapid scale is not something you need to prepare for as a top priority. There are other things you may need to worry about.

The next question is: 'Are there some good habits that are universally helpful?' We think there are. There will always be some inherent conflict between some of these habits and principles. If there is no conflict, then scaling would be a cakewalk. The trick is to make the right kind of trade-offs without losing your anchors: growth versus unit economics; speed versus being thoughtful; strong accountability versus providing support; frugality versus investing in the right capabilities; goal-orientation versus people-orientation. Juggling these habits as the game progresses without dropping the ball on any of them or losing sight of any of them is of essence. These principles need to be adapted and tweaked based on the situation on the ground and the nature of the playing field. Some unicorns will probably get built by just being at the right place at the right time. Hoping to be at the right place at the right time cannot be a strategy or a game plan. A game plan can only be about doing the right things that are in your control.

1. **Frugality is an evergreen habit:** Being frugal and spending wisely will never let you down. It is strange how even level-headed founders and leaders can go off the rails and start vanity spending after a large round of funding. Cutting back sharply when things go south is both painful and a loss of face internally. Unit economics should always be the litmus test of a business. You may choose to consciously overlook unit economics in favour of growth, especially if the battle lines are drawn around growth. But it must be a conscious decision. Be extremely frugal before the product–market fit has been established. Hire people who can multitask. Have people doing overlapping roles if needed. Do not splurge on anything. Do not hire heavyweights unless absolutely necessary.

Hire people who can punch above their weight class and those with fire in the belly. Operate out of simple and functional facilities. However, after the product–market fit is established, differentiate good costs from the bad ones as you scale. Make the right investments in people and other resources. Get tools that enhance productivity. Operate out of facilities that can get teams face time. Lease or build facilities ahead of the curve so that teams do not get randomly dispersed across multiple and suboptimal facilities. The intangible cost of this is just unbelievable. The cost of lost business can far exceed the cost of suboptimal capacity utilization. The intangible costs of having undersized leaders lead functions at this stage of growth can be high. This may not be visible very easily.

2. **Stay grounded:** All of us learn lessons in life and we should value them. What got you here may not get you there, but if you forget what got you here, you are unlikely to get anywhere. While you need to be flexible, you should remain grounded and not be carried away by what's in vogue. This is one of the true tests of character. When the new fad blows away, you will feel good about yourself and the fact that you didn't sway too much.

3. **Don't lose the ability to be hands-on:** The big picture is important but don't lose touch of the ground reality. It is common to see even the most accomplished professors teaching a basic course to first-year students at a university. This helps them stay grounded and in touch with fundamentals. This also applies to leaders in companies. Continue to stay in touch with the nuts

and bolts of the business by reviewing how the key metrics are tracking.

4. **Always start with the 'why':** It helps you define the problem better and will be your North Star when you lose direction. And you are bound to lose direction periodically! Seemingly complex issues can be settled by revisiting the 'why'. First-principles thinking is a powerful tool. One of the building blocks of first-principles thinking is starting with the 'why'. Why are we doing this? Why do customers shop with us? Simon Sinek, a prolific speaker and author, has even written a book titled 'Start with Why'.

5. **Delegate but keep track of the most important things:** It's also important to pay personal attention to these. Most of the people who claim they don't have the time are often lost in the weeds. They are busy with things that someone in their team should be doing. They have not cared to build a team, coach their team members or empower their team. As a result the important things are neglected. Or they delegate so much that it is not very different from abdication.

6. **Define your talent strategy thoughtfully:** Google might have benefitted immensely by hiring hundreds of folks from top-notch universities at top-dollar salaries, but that may not be the best strategy for you. It could also be the best strategy. Your business context and your personal beliefs are important.

7. **Cut the crap and jargon:** Technology, artificial intelligence, machine learning, deep learning and analytics are important but they are often overplayed. Don't ever stop asking basic questions, don't ever lose sight of first-principles thinking. Don't get

carried away by jargon and geekspeak. Get the experts to speak a language that anyone with some clear thinking can understand. Be optimistic but have a healthy scepticism of hype. Ask a lot of questions. Question the status quo. Ask, 'So what?' And ask what would happen if we remove some of our self-imposed constraints.

8. **Some things are just good to do:** As far as possible, define the outcomes you expect and evaluate whether your initiatives are delivering the outcomes you expected. But don't hesitate doing some fundamentally sound things even if outcomes cannot easily be measured in the short term. Treating people well, taking care of their welfare and security, creating safe work spaces and helping them do their jobs better will all qualify as fundamentally right things to do.

9. **Internal customer centricity:** Customer centricity with internal customers is as important as it is with external customers. Some of your employees serve paying customers. The rest of them must serve these employees.

10. **Avoid activity traps:** Don't sponsor events because it is a good thing to do. Don't nominate people for expensive training programmes because it is considered the right thing to do. Don't do anything because it is considered good. These things act as conversation starters or talking points in social contexts, but may not yield bang for your buck. Activity traps can sap energy and focus. So avoid activities that show you are doing something even if not doing anything may be the best thing.

Valuations and Exits: Entrepreneurs Come with Different Motives

Techstars is an American seed accelerator founded in 2006 in Boulder, Colorado. As of 2019, the company has accepted over 1600 companies into its programmes with a combined market capitalization of $18.2 billion. Less than 1 per cent of applicants are accepted. From every cohort they try and pick a start-up founded on a futuristic technology even if there is absolutely no line of sight to commercialization. 'Q Blocks' is part of the Techstars Bengaluru 2020 cohort. It is founded by two young founders one of whom, Saurabh Vij, is a particle physicist who had worked at CERN. They are bringing technology from the scientific world into the hands of everyone, and building a distributed supercomputer for companies to get access to affordable high-performance computing. They are trying to do this by connecting all the idle sources of computing in the world to build powerful supercomputers accessible from anywhere, anytime. And, in doing so, they are building the future of supercomputing. They are looking at using idle capacities of powerful graphic processing unit (GPU) based machines engaged in bitcoin mining on the one hand and the ubiquitous laptop on the other. There are serious issues to be resolved, including data privacy, but the idea, if successful, can change the landscape of computing. If you have an idea like this, don't worry about anything else. Just go and pursue your passion.

Here is another story of four co-founders whose sole motive was to create a team of high-calibre, like-minded individuals with the same passion for capital markets that they had. They were extraordinarily liberal in sharing equity with employees. Capital market was in their blood. They had all served at very senior levels in global investment banks and asset management firms. Like most entrepreneurs, they too spotted a problem and decided to fix it. Investment banks and asset management firms worldwide were faced with spiralling research costs that clients were not really willing to pay. Yet the research was essential to provide a cutting edge to the recommendations. They could do what the global IT industry had done in the past to cut costs—outsource work to lower-cost geographies. However, there was a serious problem. The IT companies offshored repetitive and/or structured work, which was never seen as providing a strategic edge. The strategic component of IT consulting continued to stay insourced. Investment research was seen as the core of investment banking and asset management. It was simply unthinkable to offshore this. Apple outsourced the manufacturing of iPhone to Foxconn in China, but the design was still the preserve of Apple headquarters at Cupertino. Offshoring research was like offshoring the Apple design. Their passion and deep knowledge of the domain created sufficient confidence for a couple of global investment banks to take the plunge!

We soon realized that making money wasn't their objective. They just seemed to be following their passion. The primary role of the chief compliance officer was to protect the interests of the company's clients and represent them within the company. This was how particular they were about protecting their interests. They had appointed independent directors to ensure that minority shareholders were taken care of, and, equally important, seen to be taken care of as well. These independent directors were compensated sufficiently so that they took their role seriously.

Corporate governance was of the highest order. They created a strong and empowered leadership team and delegated key decision-making to it. The leadership team was invited to join board meetings at fairly regular intervals and, without fail, all strategy sessions.

For the first time we were seeing a bunch of entrepreneurs whose primary aim was not to raise money or plan a spectacular exit. They were all enthusiastic professionals who derived their kick in life by working with similar high-calibre professionals and building the workplace of their dreams.

Nice people can be successful too. On a bright winter morning in December 2013, Moody's acquired 'Amba', and, in one shot, endorsed the quality of the asset that these amazing entrepreneurs had built!

In Conclusion

Bill Watterson, creator of the Calvin and Hobbes comic strip, once said, 'To invent your own life's meaning is not easy, but it's still allowed, and I think you'll be happier for the trouble.'

Scale up for the right reasons, learn along the way and hire interesting people that you would like to spend time with. Doing things the ethical way can be fun. In short, enjoy the ride!

Everything in life that seems humdrum, mundane or even stressful can actually be romantic and spectacular if you choose to look at it that way, and if you create and seed the right stories in your mind.

And, life would be delightful and breathtaking, story-like, if you are happy with who you are; if you don't desperately seek endorsement or try to always fit in; if you don't worry a lot about being judged and, at the same time, let others be without judging them. This holds true irrespective of whether you are an individual or a company.

We hope you enjoyed reading the book as much as we enjoyed writing it!

Acknowledgements

We have been wanting to put together a book like this for a while. If there was one topic that both of us understood (or at least thought we understood) reasonably well, it was about scaling start-ups. In different capacities at different points of time, in the last two decades, we have been fortunate to be part of start-ups that scaled successfully. We were equally fortunate to be associated with some truly outstanding teams and individuals from whom we learnt a great deal.

Our interests and pursuits in this domain also led us to meet several interesting and diverse sets of individuals who had a track record of building businesses in different domains. We also got to experience 'scaling' in the social sector, and some of the perspectives and learnings were absolutely fascinating, though we never developed first-hand knowledge of this. Therefore, in this book we have restricted our coverage to scaling in VC-funded start-ups, a beast that we understood well.

We had several conversations with entrepreneurs and investors to get their perspectives and listen to their stories for learnings. We would like to thank Deep Kalra of MakeMyTrip, Sanjeev Bikhchandani of Naukri, and Vishal Gupta of Bessemer Venture Partners for some interesting insights. We would also like to thank Siddhartha Ahluwalia of Prime Venture Partners for giving us access to some of his podcasts. Satej Sirur, founder of Rocketium, Sudeep Kulkarni, founder of Game Theory, Rakshit Daga, CTO at BigBasket, Bhaskar Bagchi, CEO at OLX Cash My Car, and Sidharth Rao, author of *How I Almost Blew it*, provided interesting inputs.

We are also thankful to YourStory for allowing us unfettered access to all their material and allowing us to use anything we wanted without any restriction. We have also drawn from some of the articles of ours that were published in *Mint*. We would also like to thank Malini Goyal, senior editor, *Economic Times*, for sharing her views about the start-up ecosystem in India.

Above all, we are grateful to everyone who took time out from their truly precious schedules to read the soft copy of the book and write reviews.

We would like to thank Loveleen Malhotra of Fundamentum for getting us to stick to our schedules and commitments.

We are also deeply thankful to our families for being patient and encouraging all along!

We are truly grateful to Manish Kumar, our commissioning editor at Penguin Random House, and our editor Saloni Mital. Their inputs and suggestions were extremely helpful in making the book far more readable.

Bibliography

1. Schumacher, Ernst Friedrich. *Small Is Beautiful: A Study of Economics as if People Mattered*. RHUK, 1993.
2. Tolstoy, Leo. *Anna Karenina*. Fingerprint! Publishing, 2016.
3. https://www.forbes.com/sites/kevinready/2012/08/28/a-startup-conversation-with-steve-blank/#5c74a07f0dba.
4. Ries, Eric. *The Lean Startup: How Today's Entrepreneurs Use Continuous Innovation to Create Radically Successful Businesses*. Currency, 2011.
5. https://hbr.org/1998/05/evolution-and-revolution-as-organizations-grow.
6. https://www.panasonic.com/global/corporate/history/chronicle/1932.html. Last accessed 25 April 2020.
7. https://www.aei.org/carpe-diem/fortune-500-firms-1955-v-2017-only-12-remain-thanks-to-the-creative-destruction-that-fuels-economic-prosperity/. Last accessed 25 April 2020.

8. https://www.financialexpress.com/industry/sme/
    msme-other-indias-msme-sector-swells-adds-
    these-many-enterprises-in-fy20-micro-businesses-
    dominate/1906979/.

9. https://www.jpmorganchase.com/corporate/institute/
    small-business-economic.htm.

10. Alexander, Kwame. *The Playbook: 52 Rules to Aim,
    Shoot, and Score in This Game Called Life.* HMH
    Books, 2017.

11. Prahalad, C.K. *Competing for the Future.* Harvard
    Business School Press, 1996.

12. Bahcall, Safi. *Loonshots: How to Nurture the Crazy
    Ideas that Win Wars, Cure Diseases, and Transform
    Industries.* St. Martin's Press, 2019.

13. https://www.catalyst.org/research/women-in-the-
    workforce-china/.

14. http://statisticstimes.com/economy/china-vs-india-
    economy.php.

15. West, Geoffrey. *Scale: The Universal Laws of Growth,
    Innovation, Sustainability, and the Pace of Life in
    Organisms, Cities, Economies, and Companies.*
    Penguin Books, 2018.

16. Hoffman, Reid and Chris Yeh. *Blitzscaling: The
    Lightning-Fast Path to Building Massively Valuable
    Companies.* Currency, 2018.

17. https://www.livemint.com/Companies/
    lurjUhGPebAdExiucyJeAN/Amazon-Prime-Flipkart-
    Plus-lead-ecommerce-user-base-growth.html.

18. susanjfowler.com/blog.

19. https://www.breathehr.com/blog/bro-culture-and-
    why-its-an-issue-for-startups.

20. https://www.nytimes.com/2015/08/16/technology/inside-amazon-wrestling-big-ideas-in-a-bruising-workplace.html.
21. Schein , Edgar. *The Corporate Culture Survival* Guide. Jossey-Bass, 1999.
22. https://www.businessinsider.com/author/aaron-valentic?IR=T.
23. Goldsmith, Marshal. *What Got You Here Won't Get You There: How Successful People Become Even More Successful.* Hachette Books, 2007.
24. Covey, Stephen. *The 7 Habits of Highly Effective People.* Simon & Schuster, 2019.
25. https://hbr.org/2008/02/the-founders-dilemma.
26. Collins, Jim. *Good to Great: Why Some Companies Make the Leap . . . and Others Don't.* Harper Business, 2001.
27. Carreyrou. John, *Bad Blood: Secrets and Lies in a Silicon Valley Startup.* Knopf, 2018.
28. https://www.investopedia.com/articles/personal-finance/042815/story-behind-apples-success.asp.
29. Bandyopadhyay, Tamal. *HDFC Bank 2.0.* Jaico Publishing House, 2019.
30. https://www.forbes.com/sites/anuraghunathan/2015/07/22/hdfc-banks-aditya-puri-has-created-indias-most-valuable-bank/#25ee1b0d7981.
31. https://a16z.com/2010/04/28/why-we-prefer-founding-ceos/ Andreesen Horowitz Newsletter.
32. https://a16z.com/2016/03/07/network-effects_critical-mass/ Andreesen Horowitz Newsletter.
33. https://spectrum.ieee.org/computing/networks/metcalfes-law-is-wrong.

34. https://www.history.com/news/who-invented-the-internet.
35. https://www.geeksforgeeks.org/whats-difference-internet-web/.
36. www.historyofdomainnames.com.
37. https://www.history.com/news/who-invented-the-internet.
38. https://en.wikipedia.org/wiki/Dot-com_commercials_during_Super_Bowl_XXXIV.
39. Collins, Jim and Jerry I. Porras. *Built to Last: Successful Habits of Visionary Companies.* Harper Business, 2004.
40. Rao, Sidharth. *How I Almost Blew* It. Westland, 2019.
41. https://www.cnbc.com/2019/04/03/ibm-ai-can-predict-with-95-percent-accuracy-which-employees-will-quit.html.
42. www.cs.princeton.edu.
43. https://factordaily.com/elasticity-of-human-needs-and-the-future-of-jobs/.
44. https://www.cbinsights.com/research/startup-failure-reasons-top/.
45. http://aswathdamodaran.blogspot.com/2014/06/a-disruptive-cab-ride-to-riches-uber.
46. https://www.nber.org/people/will_gornall.
47. https://techcrunch.com/2020/01/21/goldman-sachss-ceo-just-called-weworks-pulled-ipo-which-goldman-was-underwriting-proof-that-the-market-works/.
48. https://yourstory.com/2017/05/snapdeal-sins.
49. https://yourstory.com/2016/07/jabong-myntra-flipkart/.
50. https://www.linkedin.com/pulse/so-how-things-now-snapdeal-kunal-bahl/.

51. https://money.cnn.com/gallery/technology/2015/03/02/dot-com-flops/index.html.
52. https://techcrunch.com/2019/12/20/do-more-startups-die-of-indigestion-or-starvation/.
53. https://www.irishtimes.com/business/personal-finance/if-you-do-a-big-acquisition-the-odds-are-loaded-up-against-you-1.4088295.
54. Jena, Swati. *The Entrepreneur's Soulbook*. Notion Press, 2019.
55. https://techcrunch.com/2013/11/02/welcome-to-the-unicorn-club/.
56. http://leadershipconsulting.com/5-steps-becoming-effective-leader/.
57. https://www.inc.com/paul-spiegelman/employers-dont-have-the-courage-to-fire-bad-employees.html.
58. https://www.rbi.org.in/scripts/PublicationReportDetails.aspx?ID=866.
59. https://techcrunch.com/2017/05/17/heres-how-likely-your-startup-is-to-get-acquired-at-any-stage/.